# GRESLEY'S
# A4s

JOHN RYAN

GREAT NORTHERN

## ACKNOWLEDGEMENTS

I would like to thank the following people for their help: Roger Arnold, B.W.L. Brooksbank, David Burrill, John Chalcraft, Paul Chancellor, John Clayson, D.J. Dippie, David Joy, John Law, Hugh Parkin, Bill Reed, Gerald T. Robinson, Mike Sant, Andrew and Sue Warnes, Bill Wright.

---

Great Northern Books Limited
PO Box 1380, Bradford, BD5 5FB
www.greatnorthernbooks.co.uk

ISBN: 978-1-912101-99-3

Design and layout: David Burrill

CIP Data
A catalogue for this book is available from the British Library

Printed and bound in India by Replika Press Pvt. Ltd.

# CONTENTS

# INTRODUCTION

Like many railway enthusiasts, I was first introduced to the glory of steam when still a child. My father, who also had an interest, led me to Doncaster station one afternoon (around 1955) to witness the hustle and bustle of the station environs. I do not recall much about the day, yet a few vivid moments have been etched into my memory from that time. Standing on the Cattle Dock at the north end, a loud whistle made me jump and a few seconds later no. 60034 *Lord Faringdon* appeared from under the North Bridge. Glistening in the sunlight, I was immediately struck by the beauty of the locomotive and how the design stood out amongst the others at Doncaster that day. No. 60034 soon disappeared southward with a named train trailing behind, leaving a slight haze of smoke hanging over the platforms.

This first encounter with an A4 Class engine was hard to improve upon and I would only sporadically return to Doncaster station and other areas around town to watch the steam era draw to a close. I mainly developed my interest in model railways and I was extremely pleased when able to add an A4 to a modest layout in the garage. Over the years, I have built several layouts in OO Gauge and latterly O Gauge, with all prominently featuring the A4 Class working named trains of both the LNER and BR period. I am certainly not alone in my admiration for Gresley's streamlined Pacifics, as the engines created just as much of a stir when introduced in 1935 and continue to do so up to the present time.

Arguably, the A4s were Gresley's most successful design, but a lot of development went into several other classes before this was possible. The foundation was laid in the early 1920s with the introduction of the A1 Class Pacifics. Gresley had taken several years to produce this and incorporated a number of features developed over the preceding ten years, such as his '2 to 1' lever which simplified the use of three cylinders. He would doggedly stand by this, even though there were certain disadvantages, throughout his life.

The first major modification to the A1 design was the introduction of long travel valves and this improved performance and reduced coal consumption. Soon after, the boiler pressure was increased and this further improved the efficiency of the steam circuit. The fitting of diagram 94HP boilers resulted in a reclassification to A3 and new locomotives were later built with the aforementioned features. Without these changes, the introduction of the non-stop 'Flying Scotsman' express in 1928 would not have been possible. Equally as important,

the development of a corridor tender allowed a crew-change to be effected en route.

The global depression of the late 1920s/early 1930s curtailed further progress, yet Gresley was able to formulate plans for the future. These were embodied in 1934 with the introduction of P2 Class 2-8-2 no. 2001 *Cock o' the North*. The engine possessed several interesting features, including internal streamlining for steam passages, Kylchap double blastpipe and chimney, V-shaped cab front and perforated steam collector.

Gresley soon moved on to a new project. A number of railways around the world had introduced high-speed services between major cities and the London & North Eastern Railway jumped on the idea. Up to this point, many of the major expresses run by the company had been quite pedestrian and only recently had the 'Flying Scotsman' reduced the 8-hour 15-minute schedule to nearer 7½ hours. The LNER decided to introduce a high-speed train between King's Cross and Newcastle and for this Gresley was asked to design a new locomotive.

The timeframe for the completion of the project was quite restrictive, yet Gresley moved quickly and adapted the successful A3 design to the needs of the new service. This included raising the boiler pressure from 220 lb per sq. in. to 250 lb per sq. in. and adopting the relatively new concept of streamlining to reduce wind resistance, therefore saving fuel and water; the shape of the locomotive was determined in a wind tunnel.

No. 2509 *Silver Link* was the first A4 to leave Doncaster Works in early September 1935 and was worked in before the first 'Silver Jubilee' train ran at the end of the month. For the press demonstration of the service, no. 2509 was comfortably pushed to 112 mph and set the speed record for steam traction.

The train proved a success, as did the three other A4s introduced by the end of the year, and the LNER was confident that similar trains – and locomotives – would prove lucrative for the company. By the end of 1938, two new services were running – the 'Coronation' and 'West Riding Limited' – and 35 A4s were in traffic. Towards the end of the construction programme, Gresley tested the Kylchap double blastpipe and chimney with the design and four locomotives were fitted. The first was no. 4468 *Mallard* and soon after the engine achieved 125 mph on a special test and set the, still unbeaten, world speed record for steam.

With the outbreak of the Second World War, the A4s took on a new role working long, heavy trains.

The locomotives stood up to the challenge and did so amidst difficult conditions. At the end of the conflict, the class was quick to return to the distinct Garter Blue livery as a symbol of a return to normality by the LNER. Yet, track conditions stopped the reintroduction of the pre-war expresses and not until after the formation of British Railways in 1948 did similar services appear in the timetable.

As British Railways slowly formed an identity, the A4s grew back to their previous stature. Maintenance improved and reliability increased thanks to new workshop practices and components. A major boost to the class was the fitting of double blastpipe and chimneys to those not already with the equipment. Steaming troubles virtually vanished and time was cut maintaining the A4s at sheds.

Trains such as the 'Capitals Limited', 'Elizabethan' and 'Flying Scotsman', to name just a few, saw high levels of performance from the A4s. The first two mentioned trains, which took over as the summer non-stop, saw several class members accumulate large totals for journeys between the English and Scottish capitals over the season, which was a testament to the original design and subsequent improvements. The A4s were also favourites on special trains organised to celebrate events or railtours for enthusiasts up to the end of steam.

Several A4s met their fate at the end of 1962 and withdrawals progressed through to 1966. A small band of locomotives established an enclave in Scotland during this period and managed to survive on the Glasgow to Aberdeen expresses, continuing the standards established on the East Coast Main Line.

*Gresley's A4s* captures the locomotives throughout their lifetime, with over 300 excellent colour and black and white images. It falls into three distinct sections, each with members of the class portrayed in numerical order. There are photographs of every locomotive in those devoted to the LNER and BR periods. Between these two on pages 86 to 103 is a section devoted to the 1946 renumbering, which includes over a dozen A4s. This period lasted only three years, making pictures from this era particularly rare.

The A4s are shown at major centres on the East Coast Main Line, such as King's Cross station, Peterborough, Grantham, Doncaster, York, Darlington, Newcastle and Edinburgh Waverley. Also, images taken during the twilight years in Scotland are included. The surviving engines are seen at several locations in the country – Aberdeen, Glasgow and Perth.

Thankfully, six locomotives were saved from the scrapyard to represent the class for posterity. Three of these have been active on the main line in recent years, allowing new generations of enthusiasts to experience the thrill of an A4 in steam and at speed. With these engines, at the time of writing, out of service and awaiting overhaul, hopefully this fantastic collection of pictures helps to keep memories of the class alive.

*John Ryan*
*Over Peover, April 2020*

*My large O gauge layout features a great number of A4s from both the LNER and BR periods. Here, no. 2509* Silver Link *is with the 'Silver Jubilee', whilst no. 4489* Dominion of Canada *is coupled to the 'Coronation'.*

*Above* NO. 2509 – KING'S CROSS STATION

One of the premier days in the history of the LNER, and for Sir Nigel Gresley personally, was the press demonstration run of the new 'Silver Jubilee' express and the first A4 Class Pacific locomotive no. 2509 *Silver Link* on 27th September 1935. Departing from King's Cross station's platform 6 at 14.25 for Grantham, the locomotive delivered an unprecedented performance in twice reaching 112½ mph – a new world record – and maintaining high speed over a large portion of the journey. No. 2509 even succeeded in catching the 13.40 express to Harrogate, which had left King's Cross some 45 minutes earlier. Driver Taylor and Fireman Luty managed to deliver the train to Grantham in 88 minutes 15 seconds for the 105 miles, which was around the schedule, although signals and speed restrictions stopped faster running. A more leisurely pace was adopted for the return and at King's Cross Driver Taylor, who later received an MBE for his exploits, was heartily congratulated by Gresley.

### Below NO. 2509 – NEW SOUTHGATE

No. 2509 *Silver Link* had been in traffic for under a year when captured here at New Southgate working the 17.45 express from King's Cross to Harrogate. The locomotive still has the recessed streamline casing at the front end. This was changed in July 1936 following a tragic mishap at King's Cross station, where a man was killed due to insufficient clearance in this area. This flaw affected the first four locomotives and was a result of the casing projecting too far forward. Consequently, the standard drawhooks and buffers used proved too short. On the slow line (to the right) with a freight train is Gresley K3 Class 2-6-0 no. 4008.

*Opposite above* NO. 2509 – YORK

View north to York station from the Racecourse platform, as no. 2509 *Silver Link* begins the southward journey with an express from Glasgow to King's Cross during the summer of 1937. The front end is now free from the recess for the drawhook and a longer version has been installed, along with new buffers. Another addition to the front end, at the time of this modification, was the engine's number in white with shaded blue background. The size of the number was initially small on the 'silver' engines, before increased, as here, around mid-1937. York Racecourse platform, also known as Holgate Bridge, was first used in 1860 and became established in the following year. A favourite position for photographers at York, the Racecourse platforms were abandoned during the war and later demolished; the western side is currently occupied by sidings.

*Opposite below* NO. 2509 – POTTERS BAR

A contemporary postcard view of no. 2509 *Silver Link* boasts of the 'Silver Jubilee' service running at 80 mph, when reaching the top of the incline out of London at Potters Bar during the press demonstration run on 27th September 1935. The introduction of the 'Silver Jubilee' high-speed express and the exploits of the new A4s were particularly well publicised at the time and received widespread attention from enthusiasts and the general public alike. Interestingly, this postcard has been 'doctored' to remove people standing at the lineside to see the train pass and the person onboard is waving to them.

*Below* NO. 2509 – GRANTHAM STATION

A rare colour image from June 1937 shows no. 2509 *Silver Link* at the head of the southbound 'Flying Scotsman' and ready to depart from Grantham station. There are a few detail differences that can be mentioned using this picture. The handrail running along the streamlined casing was initially straight at the firebox end but has been changed subsequently, whilst the three access panels were of a larger size than used by other class members. Furthermore, the hatch closest to the cab on this side, which gave access to the Wakefield No. 7 mechanical lubricator, was covered from new on *Silver Link*, yet the panel was discarded on other engines and later on no. 2509.

"THE SILVER JUBILEE,"
TRAVELLING AT 80 MILES PER HOUR.

## NO. 2509 – KING'S CROSS STATION

No. 2509 *Silver Link* is at King's Cross station with an express during 1938. At the end of the previous year, the engine was returned to service following overhaul wearing the new Garter Blue livery and with nameplates, as well as the now standardised size buffer-level numbering.

*Above* NO. 2509 – KING'S CROSS STATION
No. 2509 has the full attention of staff in King's Cross station's locomotive yard during September 1935.

*Below* NO. 2509 – YORK SHED
Under the Mitchell Conveyor & Transport Co. 500-ton capacity mechanical coaler at York shed in the summer of 1936 is no. 2509 *Silver Link*, which has the newly modified front end; note the small number.

*Above* NO. 2510 CHALONER'S WHIN JUNCTION

Both the A4 Class locomotives and the 'Silver Jubilee' train set were developed in a relatively short time before the service was due to start. The carriages were ordered from Doncaster Works **first in** February 1935 under order no. 646 and comprised seven vehicles, with two articulated pairs and a triplet set. These were in turn split, respectively, to a third class brake, third class corridor and first class semi-open, first class brake, with the third class restaurant, kitchen car and first class restaurant contained in the triplet unit. No. 2510 *Quicksilver* has charge of the up 'Silver Jubilee' in late summer 1937 at Chaloner's Whin Junction, just south of York. This was the point where the original York & North Midland Railway line to Leeds joined the North Eastern Railway's 1871 route to Selby and Doncaster.

### Below NO. 2510 – NEWCASTLE STATION

No. 2510 *Quicksilver* was completed at Doncaster on 21st September 1935 and was present at King's Cross station for the arrival of the inaugural run of the 'Silver Jubilee' express. The locomotive was not deemed ready to work the train until three weeks later and was first noted at the head of the service on 17th October. By the end of the year, no. 2510 was transferred from King's Cross shed to Gateshead, though the allocation was only brief and a return was made at the end of January 1936. *Quicksilver* has been photographed at Newcastle Station during the year. The image shows the shorter access panels in the streamlined casing and the curved handrail at the firebox end, both of which began with no. 2510.

*Above* NO. 2510 – DONCASTER WORKS

Whilst no. 2510 *Quicksilver* is in the midst of a general repair in Doncaster Works' Crimpsall Repair Shop during March 1939, classmate no. 4500 *Garganey* has arrived to be prepared for renaming to *Sir Ronald Matthews*. No. 2510 would return to service at King's Cross in mid-April.

*Opposite above* NO. 2510 – GRANTHAM STATION

No. 2510 *Quicksilver* has backed on to a southbound express at Grantham around mid-1938/1939. The engine now has Garter Blue livery and cast nameplate.

*Opposite below* NO. 2510 – NEW SOUTHGATE

The LNER's modern A4 Pacific presents a sharp contrast to an old London Midland & Scottish Railway 0-6-0T at New Southgate. No. 2510 *Quicksilver* is the engine and has a down 'Silver Jubilee' express.

*Below* NO. 2510 – DONCASTER WORKS

No. 2510 *Quicksilver* has been pulled out of the paint shop into the yard at Doncaster Works for the official photograph in September 1935; note the missing piece of streamline casing to provide access to the mechanical lubricators.

*Opposite above* NO. 2511 – DARLINGTON

Although two A4 Pacifics were in traffic by the end of September 1935, there was a break of six weeks before the third locomotive of the original four ordered was put into service from Doncaster Works. No. 2511 *Silver King* spent two weeks at King's Cross before being transferred to Gateshead, where the engine became the standby for the 'Silver Jubilee' engine if a failure occurred. In testament to the high reliability of the service, no. 2511 *Silver King* was the least used of the 'silver' engines on the 'Silver Jubilee' and amassed only eighty journeys from the 1,952 trains that ran between King's Cross and Newcastle over a four-year period. Alternative employment has been found for the locomotive, being a rather mundane freight formed from a large number of vans, but also some cattle wagons and containers. No. 2511 is just a short distance north of Darlington station travelling southward.

*Opposite below* NO. 2511

An early image of no. 2511 *Silver King* at an unidentified location. The four 'silver' locomotives received new corridor tenders when built and these were fitted in sequence, 5589-5592. They were slightly modified from the original 1928 corridor tenders, mainly concerning the appearance to conform with the streamlining of the locomotive. Originally, plating partially enclosed the coal space and covered the area at the rear around the water filler cap which reduced the coal capacity to 8 tons.

*Below* NO. 2511 – EDINBURGH HAYMARKET SHED

No. 2511 *Silver King* passes Edinburgh Haymarket shed with a train, likely during the first half of 1936. For most of July of that year the engine was in Doncaster Works for modifications to be carried out on the front end.

### *Opposite above* NO. 2511 – DARLINGTON

No. 2511 *Silver King* was the last of the four 'silver' A4s to be repainted with the Garter Blue livery, when the transformation was undertaken at Doncaster Works over two months ending in early August 1938. The first had been no. 2512 *Silver Fox* in November 1937, followed by no. 2509 *Silver Link* (December) and no. 2510 *Quicksilver* in May 1938. No. 2511 is working the 'Flying Scotsman' service, likely during 1939, just north of Darlington.

### *Opposite below* NO. 2511 – POTTERS BAR

The northbound 'Silver Jubilee' express has just reached the summit of the eight-mile incline of 1 in 200 from Hornsey to Potters Bar on 17th June 1936. No. 2511 *Silver King* is the A4 leading the service which was booked around a mile-a-minute for this section. The A4s had no problem gaining speed over this part of the line, despite the gradient and the 220 tons behind the tender.

### *Below* NO. 2511 – CROFT SPA STATION

View north at Croft Spa station in early summer 1936, as no. 2511 *Silver King* rushes southward with an early evening express. The engine was around a month away from entering Doncaster Works for the front end modification. This would be the engine's second return to the shops following a light repair earlier in the year and another trip would be made there before the end of 1936 for the first general repair. Croft Spa station, which was the first on the ECML over the border between Yorkshire and County Durham, was opened by the Stockton & Darlington Railway in March 1841 as Croft. Before the end of the 19th century the name was changed to Croft Spa and the station was closed with this title in 1969, although local services, apart from those to Richmond, had ceased nearly a decade earlier.

*Opposite above* NO. 2512 – KING'S CROSS SHED

Whilst at first glance this image shows no. 2512 *Silver Fox* on the turntable at King's Cross shed, the picture was specifically taken to illustrate the addition of new vacuum turning gear. As part of a major upgrade of facilities undertaken at King's Cross shed during the early 1930s, a 70 ft turntable replaced a 54 ft example which had been installed earlier in the century. The 70 ft turntable (from Ransomes & Rapier) was located in the north east corner of the site, near the entrance off the main line, which is seen in the background under York Way bridge. As evidenced here, the turntable was originally hand operated and the changeover to the Cowans Sheldon vacuum turning gear (surely to the relief of many firemen) was made around 1936, with this photograph dating from 1st August.

*Opposite below* NO. 2512 – MARSHMOOR

No. 2512 *Silver Fox* heads a southbound 'Silver Jubilee' express at Marshmoor (between Hatfield and Brookmans Park on the East Coast Main Line) on 9th June 1937. The engine had around 15 miles left to run and, after tackling a relatively gentle rise from Brookmans Park to Potters Bar, much of this was easy going to King's Cross.

*Below* NO. 2512 – DONCASTER WORKS

Inside the Paint Shop at Doncaster Works, likely during the late 1930s, is no. 2512 *Silver Fox*. The locomotive was the first of the four 'silver' locomotives to receive the new Garter Blue livery in November 1937 at the end of the engine's first general repair. No. 2512 also had the nameplates fitted to the side of the streamlined casing. Doncaster's Paint Shop dated from 1902 and was erected as part of a large-scale expansion to the west of the original site on the Crimpsall meadows. The Paint Shop was located in the south east corner and the building had a northlight roof covering eight roads with shallow pits; each of the tracks could accommodate five locomotives.

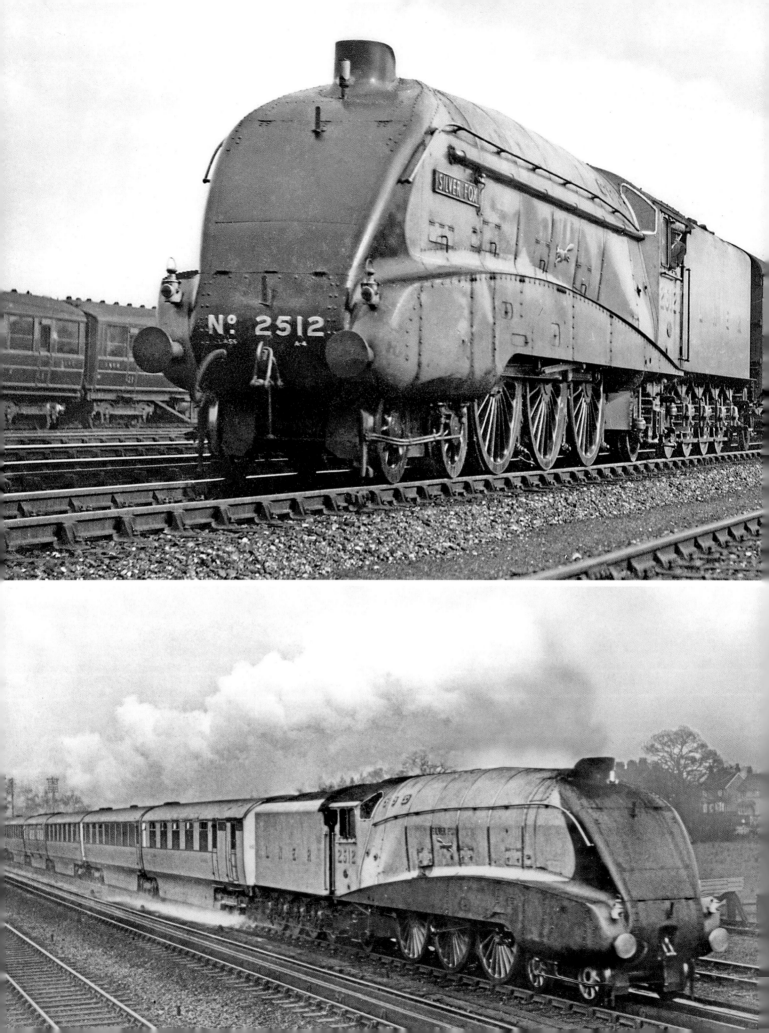

*Opposite above* NO. 2512 – NEW SOUTHGATE

Seven miles out from King's Cross station, no. 2512 *Silver Fox* is pulling an express to Leeds up the 1 in 200 to Potters Bar.

*Opposite below* NO. 2512

Taking water at an unidentified set of water troughs is no. 2512 *Silver Fox*. The LNER had six sets on the East Coast Main Line. Four were on the ex-Great Northern Railway section – Langley, Werrington, Muskham and Scrooby – whilst two belonged to the ex-North Eastern Railway section – Wiske and Lucker. No. 2512 was first used on the 'Silver Jubilee' service on 3rd January 1936 and went on to complete 409 journeys with the train; only one failure was recorded against the engine. Of the total 1,952 'Silver Jubilee' services, just 16 failures happened over four years and on average one occurred every 32,726½ miles.

*Below* NO. 2512 – DONCASTER WORKS

No. 2512 *Silver Fox* was completed at Doncaster Works on 18th December 1935 with works number 1823. From new, no. 2512 carried embellishments that were unique to the locomotive. The most recognisable was the pair of silver foxes – one fitted to each side of the locomotive, originally under the name – donated to the engine by steel manufacturers Samuel Fox & Co. of Sheffield. No. 2512 also possessed stainless steel boiler bands. The engine ran with the short buffers and drawhook until October 1936 when the longer type was used; at this time the large version of the front number was applied, with the revised version appearing when no. 2512 was repainted a year later.

*Above* NO. 4482 – PETERBOROUGH STATION

No. 4482 *Golden Eagle* has been given the mundane task of hauling a local service around 1937 and is with the train at Peterborough station.

*Opposite above* NO. 4482 – EDINBURGH HAYMARKET

Running past Edinburgh Haymarket shed is no. 4482 *Golden Eagle*. The locomotive is coupled to an express from Aberdeen, although pre-war the A4s generally worked only as far as Dundee.

*Opposite below* NO. 4482 – GRANTHAM

The fireman of no. 4482 *Golden Eagle* looks ready to turn the 125-ton (approx.) A4 at Grantham during the mid-1930s.

*Below* NO. 4482 – BERWICK-UPON-TWEED

Crossing the Royal Border Bridge, Berwick-upon-Tweed, with the 'Flying Scotsman' express during 1939 is no. 4482 *Golden Eagle*.

*Above* NO. 4483

The design of the front end of the A4 was inspired by the Bugatti petrol railcar used on the Paris-Deauville route by the État (State) Railway. Gresley had personally travelled in the railcar with his assistant O.V.S. Bulleid and Ettore Bugatti himself. The latter had been originally involved in the construction of luxury motor vehicles and racing cars before being forced to diversify with the railcar. Inevitably, he took the lead from the road and used four car engines, amounting to some 800 horsepower, to provide traction for the railcar and a top speed of 100 mph was possible. Bugatti had previously reached a speed of 107 mph on the road with the Type 32 race car of 1923 and this had also utilised a wedge-shaped design at the front end. Another new form of transport to influence Gresley was the aeroplane, particularly the aerofoil (or wing), which was incorporated into the design of the running plate and side skirts. He was quite sure of the line he wanted this to take and when he saw that his vision was being interpreted incorrectly at Doncaster Works during the construction of no. 2509 *Silver Link*, he immediately had the drawing office improve the design. No. 4483 *Kingfisher* is at an unidentified location (possibly Edinburgh Haymarket) during the late 1930s. The locomotive has the front end opened to allow access to the smokebox during servicing and this was possible through a crank inserted through the casing at a point above the centre of the bogie and just in front of the cylinders.

*Opposite above* NO. 4483 – NEWCASTLE STATION

No. 4483 *Kingfisher* was the first new A4 to be based at Haymarket shed, Edinburgh, and arrived there in late 1936. In 1937, several more class members presented themselves at the depot, particularly for the inauguration of the 'Coronation' express, but also the non-stop 'Flying Scotsman' during the summer. When not working either of these duties, the A4s were regularly used on normal expresses as far as Newcastle, in addition to trains for Glasgow and to Dundee with services for Aberdeen. No. 4483, which stands at the head of an unidentified southbound express at Newcastle during the late 1930s, was six months at Haymarket from new though transferred to King's Cross for six months from July 1937 only to return north of the border early in 1938.

*Opposite below* NO. 4483 – EDINBURGH HAYMARKET SHED

At Edinburgh Haymarket shed in 1937 is no. 4483 *Kingfisher*. The engine has the original LNER green livery applied, with black covering the front casing section, and this was the case for the first year in service before a change was made to Garter Blue in January 1938.

*Below* NO. 4484

No. 4484 *Falcon* only wore the LNER green livery for ten months from new in February 1937 until the first general repair which was carried out in November/December. The engine is at an unidentified location, although being Haymarket-allocated at this time, the shed could be a candidate.

*Bottom* NO. 4484 – SHEPRETH

No. 4484 *Falcon* heads a short train of empty coaching stock towards the East Coast Main Line on 31st July 1943. The engine had started the journey at Cambridge and has been captured a relatively short distance from there at Shepreth. No. 4484 has wartime black livery applied with valances over the wheels removed and the abbreviated 'NE' on the tender.

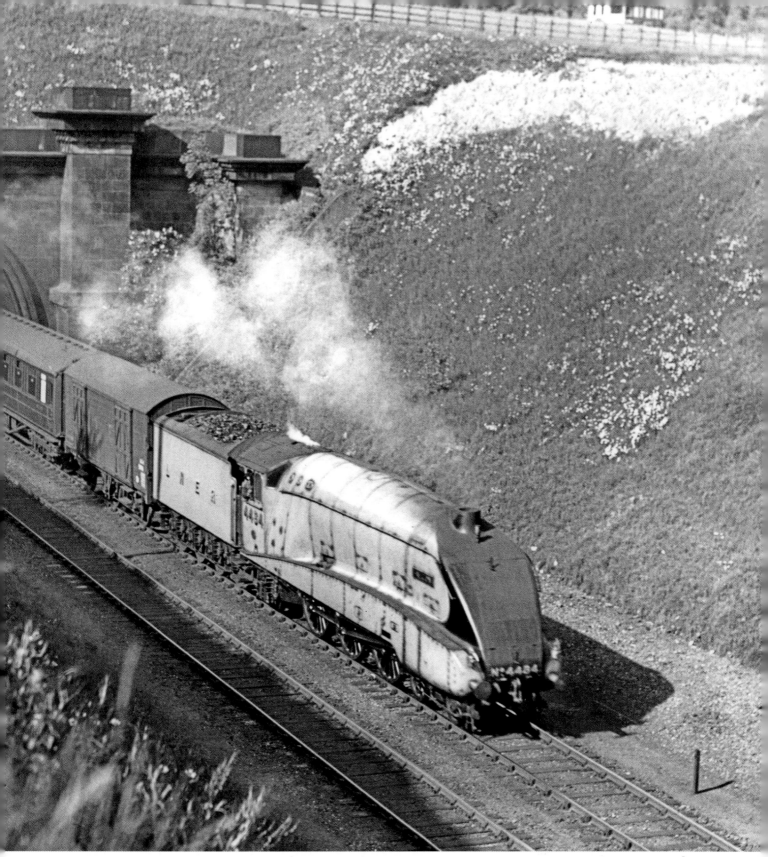

*Above* NO. 4484 – WELWYN NORTH STATION

View north from the embankment a short distance away from Welwyn North station, as no. 4484 *Falcon* emerges from the portal of Welwyn South Tunnel on 8th June 1939. Just the first carriage of the Edinburgh to King's Cross express is visible, with the remainder trailing behind in the 446-yard long tunnel. The locomotive was a recent addition to the number of A4s at King's Cross shed following a transfer from Haymarket in March.

*Opposite above* NO. 4485 – POTTERS BAR

When the 17 general service A4s were ordered in January 1936, the decision was taken to discontinue the use of silver/grey for the livery. This led to a return to the traditional LNER green, with black and white lining, for no. 4482 *Golden Eagle* when the engine entered traffic in late December 1936. A further five locomotives, up to no. 4487 *Sea Eagle*, also received green livery, yet an alteration was made to the front end, where the black extended back to the first clothing band of the boiler, creating a unique appearance. The reasoning behind this was the paint was not thought to be able to withstand the heat present at the smokebox end and could crack and blister. No instances appear to have been recorded of this happening with no. 4482, yet the decision was soon made to remove the LNER green livery and replace with the new Garter Blue when the engines concerned passed through Doncaster for repair. No. 4485 *Kestrel* only had the livery until the end of 1937 and has been pictured during the middle of the year working the 'Flying Scotsman' express at Potters Bar.

*Opposite below* NO. 4485

A particularly unclean no. 4485 *Kestrel* is at an undisclosed location during the late 1930s. Note the open inspection covers that allow the driver to oil motion components.

*Below* NO. 4485 – NEWCASTLE STATION

A night-time study of no. 4485 *Kestrel*, captured in 1938, as the locomotive stands at the head of an express at Newcastle station that is destined for Edinburgh. The engine was a resident of Haymarket depot at this time and had returned there following a sojourn at Gateshead from early October 1937 to late January 1938, although much of this period was spent in Doncaster Works for a general overhaul. No. 4485 transferred to King's Cross in March 1939 and remained in England until the early 1960s.

*Opposite above* NO. 4486 – DARLINGTON

Travelling northward away from Darlington in the late 1930s is no. 4486 *Merlin*. The locomotive is with a 'Newcastle Chronicle Excursion', which could be one of several organised by the newspaper over the summer months throughout the 1930s. This had been done in partnership with the LNER and took holidaymakers to various locations across the country, including London, Scotland, Wales, East Anglia, Lake District, Yorkshire Coast, etc. Prices ranged from 18s to over £6 for several days in Jersey.

*Opposite below* NO. 4486 – DONCASTER WORKS

One of the more unusual events in the history of the A4 Class occurred at Doncaster Works in the summer of 1944. Recently appointed director of the LNER FitzHerbert Wright, who replaced Lord Burleigh, arranged for no. 4486 *Merlin*, which was in Doncaster Works for a general overhaul, to carry the name and birth date of his children, Brigid, Bryan and Davinia. Here the locomotive has the latter's details, though a mistake has been made with the name 'Davina'; the birth date is correct. FitzHerbert Wright's youngest child Susan was not included in the naming ceremony for some unknown reason. The locomotive subsequently returned to traffic as no. 4486 *Merlin*.

*Below* NO. 4486 – EDINBURGH HAYMARKET SHED

A fair-sized chunk of coal has been taken out of the tender of no. 4486 *Merlin*, which has returned to Edinburgh Haymarket shed for servicing, following the completion of an unknown duty. To simplify access for maintaining the Gresley '2 to 1' lever, a hinged panel was fitted in front of the cylinders from early 1939 and this stopped the need to remove the entire panel. No. 4486 has the modification, which could have been carried out during the engine's general repair in late spring 1939.

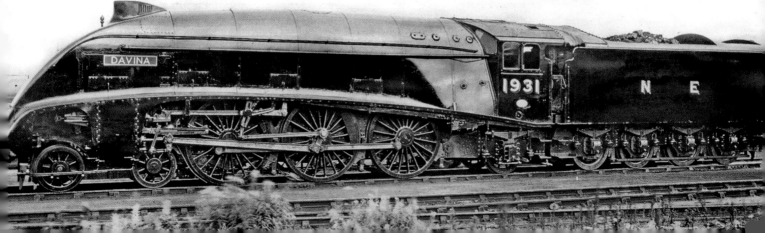

*Above* NO. 4487 – BURNMOUTH

For around 13 miles, the East Coast Main Line runs along the coastline between Beal and Burnmouth. This stretch of the route also includes the crossing of the border between England and Scotland. No. 4487 *Sea Eagle* heads a northbound 'Flying Scotsman' express in the area, just south of Burnmouth during August 1939. The non-stop service had started that year on 3rd July with no. 4484 *Falcon* leading the train away from Edinburgh Waverley station, whilst the final non-stop 'Flying Scotsman' ran on 31st August before the declaration of war halted proceedings for several years.

*Opposite above* NO. 4487 – DONCASTER WORKS

No. 4487 *Sea Eagle* stands particularly resplendent inside the Paint Shop at Doncaster Works around early March 1937, just before entering traffic. The engine was the final A4 to have the LNER green livery with extended black front section applied and no. 4487 ran in this condition until February 1938.

*Opposite below* NO. 4487 – KING'S CROSS STATION

Only briefly allocated to Edinburgh Haymarket shed when new, no. 4487 *Sea Eagle* was transferred southward to Gateshead depot and was employed there until February 1938. Here, the engine stands with a northbound express before departing from King's Cross station during 1937.

*Above* NO. 4488 – YORK SHED

With the decision made to introduce a second high-speed service and the start date approaching, the uncertainty over the A4 Class livery had to be resolved. The LNER ultimately followed the example of the 'Silver Jubilee' and chose a colour representative of the occasion, which in this instance was the coronation of George VI. Garter Blue was in use as part of the celebrations and was adopted for the A4s specially chosen to haul the new high speed express. The colour covered most of the engine and tender, with the front again black, and lining of red and white was used, both bands being ¼ in. wide, whilst the wheel centres were a shade of maroon. Further embellishment was added by polished metal trim to the skirting over both the coupled wheels and tender wheels, as well as polished metal cabside numbers and 'LNER' on the tender sides. The front number ceased to be applied with shaded transfer numbers and lettering, being instead painted on by hand in silver. No. 4488 *Union of South Africa* suitably illustrates the new livery at York shed during 1938.

*Opposite above* NO. 4488 – NEWCASTLE STATION

After several months in operation, the 'Silver Jubilee' had proved to be a worthwhile endeavour for the LNER. This was thanks, not just to the prestige and publicity generated, but to the money accrued through day-to-day service; the supplementary fares alone had produced £12,000. Chief General Manager of the LNER, Sir Ralph Wedgwood, authorised a new high-speed express in mid-1936 to begin service during the following year. This was to run between King's Cross and Edinburgh Waverley stations, departing at 16.00 and 16.30 respectively. Six hours were allowed for the journey, including stops at York northward and Newcastle for the southbound train. The locomotive was required to maintain an average speed of 65.5 mph to keep to the schedule with the 312-ton train, which was slightly lower than that required by the 'Silver Jubilee' service. As George VI ascended to the throne during 1937, the new train was called the 'Coronation' and first travelled between the capitals on 5th July. No. 4488 *Union of South Africa* has just made the stop at Newcastle with the train during the late 1930s.

*Opposite below* NO. 4488 – SANDY

No. 4488 *Union of South Africa* was completed at Doncaster Works in mid-April 1937, but was held back as the engine was used to determine a new livery. At this time, the locomotive was named *Osprey*, though when ready for service in late June no. 4488 was *Union of South Africa*, as names of dominions of the British Empire were chosen to reflect the theme of the coronation. The nameplates of the five engines specifically allocated to the new train were chromium plated and the background was red. No. 4488 is working a northbound 'Coronation' express during 1939 at Sandy, 44 miles from King's Cross.

*Above* NO. 4489 – KING'S CROSS STATION
Sir Nigel Gresley stands in the cab of no. 4489 *Dominion of Canada*, as the High Commissioner of that country, Vincent Massey, takes the regulator to drive the engine to the end of the platform 6 at King's Cross station on 15th June 1937. The locomotive had been the subject of a naming ceremony; the other 'Coronation' engines were similarly honoured during the period.

*Below* NO. 4489 – STOKE SUMMIT
A freight train has been diverted into sidings at Stoke Summit (south of Grantham) so no. 4489 *Dominion of Canada* can pass with the 'Flying Scotsman' during June 1938.

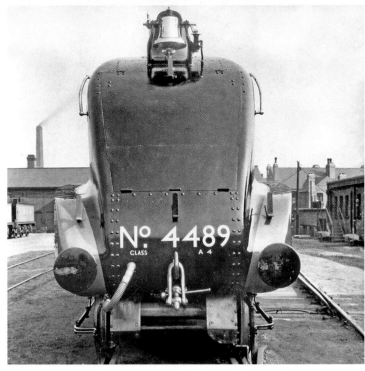

*Above and Right* NO. 4489 – DONCASTER WORKS
The Canadian Pacific Railway gifted the LNER a bell, similar to the type used by the company's locomotives, in early 1938 and this was subsequently installed on no. 4489 *Dominion of Canada* at Doncaster Works (shown here). Photograph on right courtesy Mike Sant.

*Below* NO. 4489 – KING'S CROSS STATION
Crowds have gathered to witness the press demonstration of the new 'Coronation' train on 30th June 1937. No. 4489 *Dominion of Canada* was given the honour of working the service and during the return down Stoke Bank an attempt was made to reach the British speed record, although, disappointingly, only 109 mph was achieved. Photograph courtesy Mike Sant.

*Opposite above* NO. 4490

No. 4490 *Empire of India* was completed at Doncaster in June 1937 as works no. 1855. The engine is working an express at an unidentified location during the late 1930s.

*Opposite below* NO. 4490 – KING'S CROSS SHED

The Gresley A4 benefitted from several developments of the original A1/A3 Pacific design from the early 1920s. No. 4490 *Empire of India* stands in front of King's Cross shed when nearly new in July 1937 with Gresley A3 no. 4480 *Enterprise* for company.

*Below* NO. 4490 – DONCASTER STATION

The southbound 'Flying Scotsman' passes through Doncaster station, likely at reduced speed due to the work being carried out on the left, in the late 1930s, with no. 4490 *Empire of India* at the head of the train. Initially allocated to King's Cross shed, the locomotive transferred to Edinburgh Haymarket in March 1938 and became a long-term resident at the depot.

*Opposite above* NO. 4491 – KING'S CROSS STATION

A small gathering has formed at the end of a platform at King's Cross station to witness the departure of no. 4491 *Commonwealth of Australia* with a northbound 'Coronation' service during summer 1937. Allocated to Edinburgh Haymarket from new, no. 4491 was a particular favourite of the shed for use on the 'Coronation' during the first summer. This began with the locomotive being rostered to work the first northbound service from King's Cross on 5th July with Driver Dron and Fireman Charlton from Gateshead on the footplate. Of the 51 journeys made from this date, no. 4491 was at the head of the train on 48 occasions, completing 18,864 miles. As a testament to the durability of the design, no. 4491 did not subsequently receive works attention until May 1938. A slight problem did see no. 4491 record the first failure of a locomotive on the 'Coronation', as the engine was removed at Newcastle on 16th September and A3 no. 2597 *Cicero* substituted; the latter only lost a minute on the scheduled time.

*Opposite below* NO. 4491 – DONCASTER WORKS

No. 4491 *Commonwealth of Australia* as new at Doncaster Works in June 1937.

*Below* NO. 4491 – KING'S CROSS SHED

No. 4491 *Commonwealth of Australia* was dispatched from Doncaster Works in mid-June 1937 for the formal naming ceremony at King's Cross station, which took place on 18th June conducted by Mr S.M. Bruce, High Commissioner. Traditional practice for those engines being specially named was for the plates to be covered until the event and this is the case here with no. 4491, as the engine waits in the yard at King's Cross shed. During the modernisation work carried out at the depot in the 1930s, the 500-ton mechanical coaler (seen in the background) was installed to replace a coal stage. At the time, the latter was said to be dispensing over 1,500 tons of coal weekly to the engines working from King's Cross.

*Opposite above* NO. 4492 – RETFORD
An excursion to Retford was organised to allow the Doncaster Works photographer to capture this official picture of no. 4492 *Dominion of New Zealand* with the 'Coronation' carriages shortly before the train went into service. The 'Coronation' was different from the 'Silver Jubilee' in seating arrangements and the omission of the restaurant cars to boost passenger capacity, as meals were served at seats which was an innovation in itself. The colour scheme was similarly bold and consisted of Marlborough Blue for the upper panels and Garter Blue for the lower. An observation car was provided for use in the summer months, although missing here.

*Opposite below* NO. 4492 – KING'S CROSS SHED
Whilst on the turntable at King's Cross shed, no. 4492 *Dominion of New Zealand* and the driver take time to pose for the camera. The date is pre-March 1939 as the original Crosby Tri-Note whistle is still fitted, whereas after this time the engine used a whistle presented by the New Zealand Government Railway.

*Below* NO. 4492 – WELWYN NORTH STATION
View northward from Welwyn North station, as no. 4492 *Dominion of New Zealand* approaches at speed with a King's Cross-bound express from Harrogate and Leeds on 17th September 1938.

*Opposite above* NO. 4493 – WELWYN NORTH STATION

The 08.55 express from Glasgow Queen Street to King's Cross rushes southward through Welwyn North station on 17th September 1938 and no. 4493 *Woodcock* is leading this Saturday-only train. No. 4493 was built at Doncaster Works in July 1937 and continued the order for general service A4s, whilst a reversion was made to LNER green livery as applied to no. 4482 *Golden Eagle*. The name *Woodcock* also carried the theme of birds of fast or powerful flight – as specially chosen by Gresley himself – although this had previously adorned no. 4489 *Dominion of Canada* when the engine first went into traffic and has been reused. No. 4493 received Garter Blue livery in July 1938.

*Opposite below* NO. 4493

No. 4493 *Woodcock* was initially allocated to Gateshead shed and spent six months there before moved to Doncaster depot. Only employed for a month, during February 1938, no. 4493 was taken on at King's Cross and remained there for five years. The engine is at an unidentified location with an express during the locomotive's first year in service, as LNER green is still in use.

*Below* NO. 4493 – NEW SOUTHGATE

In stark contrast to the care and attention bestowed on the A4 Class before the Second World War, no. 4493 *Woodcock* carries the dirt and grime of a hard-worked engine. The image dates from April 1946 and no. 4493 is at the head of the 16.00 service from King's Cross to Leeds, passing through New Southgate. The locomotive had last been at Doncaster Works for overhaul in September 1945 – the side skirting had been removed some three years earlier – and would be under attention again in May 1947.

*Above* NO. 4494 – NEW SOUTHGATE

Director of the LNER and Chairman of the Locomotive Committee Andrew K. McCosh was honoured by having his name carried by an A4 from August 1942, with no. 4494 being christened. The locomotive has a service to Leeds here at New Southgate in July 1946.

*Opposite above* NO. 4494 – KING'S CROSS STATION

No. 4494 began life at Doncaster Works in mid-August 1937 as *Osprey*, which had been briefly assigned to no. 4488 *Union of South Africa*. No. 4494 is coupled to a train at King's Cross station within the first year of service.

*Opposite below* NO. 4494

No. 4494 *Osprey* is engaged on an express service at an unidentified location during 1937/1938. The engine had LNER green livery applied from new until October 1938, when the only A4 still running in this condition. Although no. 4494 was Grantham-allocated at this time, the engine had started service at Heaton, before moving to Doncaster in January 1938 and reaching Grantham in April.

*Opposite above* NO. 4495 – WOOLMER GREEN

Although not the 'West Riding Limited', no. 4495 *Golden Fleece* is travelling with another express from Leeds bound for King's Cross on 11th June 1938. The train is at Woolmer Green, a short distance to the south of Stevenage.

*Opposite below* NO. 4495 – DONCASTER STATION

As with the 'Silver Jubilee' and 'Coronation' expresses, the LNER made the decision to allocate dedicated, specially named locomotives to the 'West Riding Limited'. Yet, this appears to have been made quite late in the day. No. 4495 *Great Snipe* was completed at Doncaster Works at the end of August and was in traffic for nearly two weeks, before recalled for repainting and renaming to *Golden Fleece*. The locomotive has LNER green livery and original name here at Doncaster station on 4th September when being run in with an express.

*Below* NO. 4495 – LEEDS CENTRAL STATION

Planned in tandem with the 'Coronation' express service, the 'West Riding Limited' started some two months later at the end of September 1937. The train ran between King's Cross, Leeds and Bradford, with departure from the north scheduled at 11.33 and the capital 19.10. A press demonstration of the 'West Riding Limited', which had coaching stock strikingly similar to the 'Coronation', was scheduled for Thursday, 23rd September, journeying from Leeds to Barkston, just north of Grantham. No. 4495 *Golden Fleece* stands at the head of this train at Leeds Central station, with invited guests inspecting the carriages and locomotive before departure. Closest to camera is R.A. Thom, Mechanical Engineer, Doncaster.

*Above* NO. 4496 – KING'S CROSS STATION
A study of the cab of no. 4496 *Golden Shuttle*, taken when the engine was at King's Cross station. Note the metal numbers and lettering in the Gill Sans style.

*Opposite above* NO. 4496 – WELWYN GARDEN CITY
A southbound 'West Riding Limited' service passes Welwyn Garden City behind no. 4496 *Golden Shuttle*.

*Opposite below* NO. 4496 – DONCASTER WORKS
At Doncaster Works and ready to enter traffic in early September 1937 is no. 4496 *Golden Shuttle*. The locomotive was initially based in the town, but only for ten days before taking a berth at King's Cross to begin working the 'West Riding Limited'.

*Below* NO. 4496 – PETERBOROUGH SHED
No. 4496 *Golden Shuttle* at Peterborough shed during June 1946 as renamed *Dwight D. Eisenhower* during the previous year.

*Above* NO. 4497 – EDINBURGH HAYMARKET SHED

No. 4497 *Golden Plover* continued the theme of bird names following the brief break to name the 'West Riding Limited' engines with two related to the textile industry of the area. Completed at Doncaster in early October 1937, the engine was delivered new a short time afterwards to Edinburgh Haymarket, where no. 4497 has been pictured during the late 1930s about to take on water. As with other A4s at the depot, *Golden Plover* was worked hard and in early 1939 was noted as being used on the 'Coronation' exclusively for over six weeks, recording an impressive total of 15,327 miles over the period.

*Opposite* NO. 4497 – DONCASTER WORKS

A special project undertaken at Doncaster Works in 1937 was the creation of an exhibition train for Pilkington Glass, which had a large factory locally. Two ex-dining cars were refurbished to display numerous glass products and the carriages were then transported around the country to visit 39 towns and cities. Following completion at Doncaster, the carriages have been posed with new A4 no. 4497 *Golden Plover*.

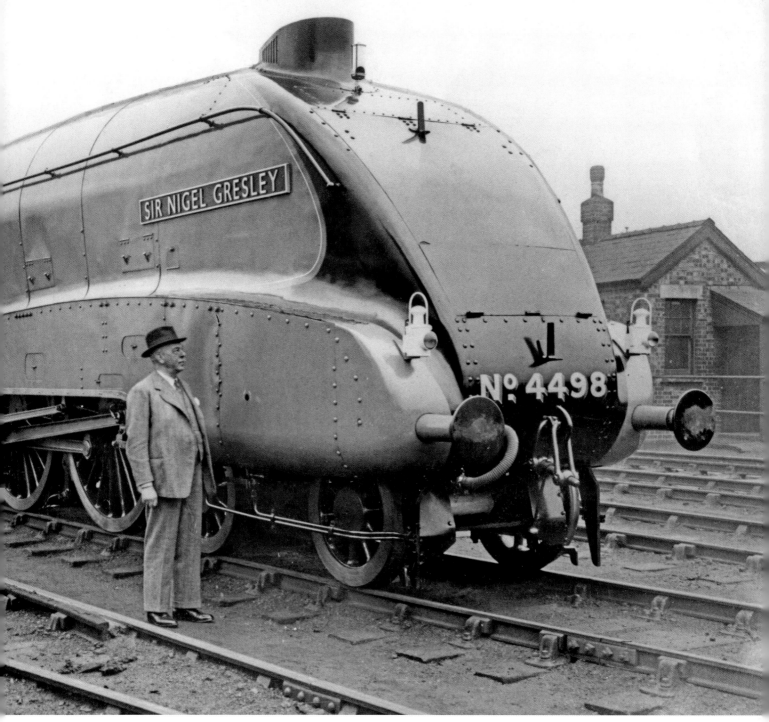

*Above* NO. 4498 – KING'S CROSS SHED

An enthusiast and historian of the LNER, K. Risdon Prentice, realised that no. 4498 would be the 100th Gresley Pacific when completed at Doncaster in late 1937. He suggested to the authorities that this should carry the name of the locomotives' famous designer which was enthusiastically accepted. An official naming ceremony was carried out at Marylebone station on 27th November 1937 and Sir Nigel Gresley (knighted 1936) is with no. 4498 at King's Cross around this time.

*Opposite above* NO. 4498 – STEVENAGE NORTH STATION

To celebrate the introduction of a new set of carriages for the 'Flying Scotsman' train in 1938, the LNER arranged for the service of 1888 to be assembled to mark the occasion. Great Northern Railway Stirling 'Single' no. 1 was also restored to be able to take the vintage train on a journey from King's Cross to Stevenage, where the guests transferred to the new set hauled by no. 4498 *Sir Nigel Gresley*.

*Opposite below* NO. 4498 – WOOD GREEN STATION

View north at Wood Green station in 1938, as no. 4498 *Sir Nigel Gresley* approaches with the 'Flying Scotsman'. Although not originally fitted with metal numbers and lettering, these embellishments were added from early 1939. The front number was unique from new, being in silver with blue shading rather than the standard gold and red.

*Above* NO. 4462

'On shed' at an unidentified location during the late 1930s is no. 4462 *Great Snipe*. Initially allocated to King's Cross, the engine had spells at Gateshead and Heaton before settling at Haymarket in mid-1941.

*Opposite above* NO. 4462 – NEW SOUTHGATE

A northbound express travels through New Southgate during 1938 with no. 4462 *Great Snipe* leading the way.

*Opposite below* NO. 4462 – DONCASTER WORKS

On 5th June 1941, no. 4462 *Great Snipe* was at Doncaster Works with no streamlined skirting, which was to be removed as an aid to maintenance; note the brackets are still in place.

*Below* NO. 4462 – DONCASTER WORKS

A few weeks after the photograph 'Opposite below' was taken at Doncaster Works, no. 4462 had undergone a general repair. In the meantime the authorities chose to retain the streamlined skirting in front of the cylinders, although the shedmaster at Edinburgh soon dispensed with these pieces. *Great Snipe* had also been replaced by the name *William Whitelaw* in honour of the Chairman of the LNER (1923-1938).

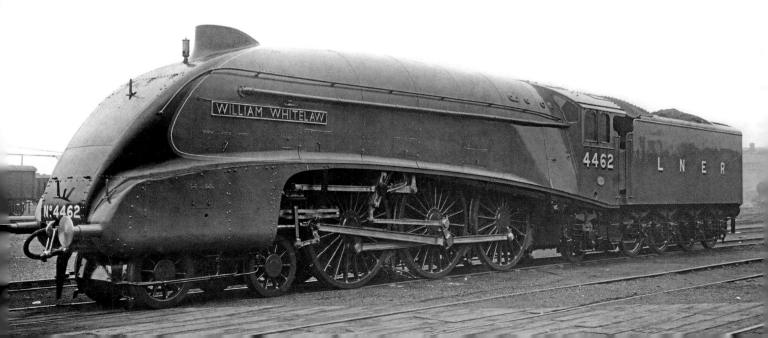

*Above* NO. 4463 – HADLEY WOOD

By the end of 1936, further A4s were considered necessary and orders were placed at Doncaster for new locomotives. A total of 14 emerged from the shops before the end of 1938, bringing the class total at that time to 35 A4s. There was a break of only a month between the appearance of no. 4498 *Sir Nigel Gresley* and no. 4462 *Great Snipe*, yet the works numbers continued in sequence, even if the outward numbering did not. The constituents of the LNER generally did not closely follow ordering to numbering schemes and little changed with the new company. Engines built under the auspices of the LNER mostly fitted in the gaps left in the constituents' stock lists. The 17 A4s erected in 1936/1937 followed this pattern, although the situation could have been quite erratic if the original numbers allocated found their way to the intended locomotives. With the introduction of 14 new A4s beginning late 1937, a continuous sequence was unavailable and the numbers were eventually spread over several gaps, with the largest being nos 4462-4469, which fell between the last Ivatt C1 Class 4-4-2 Atlantic and the first Gresley A1 Pacific, no. 4470 *Great Northern*. The second number, no. 4463, was taken by works no. 1865, *Sparrow Hawk*, when the locomotive entered service in late November 1937. Here, the engine has a northbound express at Hadley Wood in 1938.

*Opposite* NO. 4463 – GANWICK

No. 4463 *Sparrow Hawk*'s first allocation was to Gateshead shed and by the following year was one of eight A4s employed there. Although the King's Cross and Edinburgh Haymarket engines dominated the 'Silver Jubilee' and 'Coronation' high-speed trains, a Gateshead engine was used frequently on the 'Flying Scotsman' between Newcastle and King's Cross. No. 4463 has an express for King's Cross during 1938 and is between Potters Bar tunnel (just glimpsed on the extreme left) and Hadley Wood tunnel at Ganwick.

*Above* NO. 4464 – THIRSK

The East Coast Main Line between York and Darlington was quite straight and level for the 44 miles, allowing many locomotives to reach and maintain high speeds. No. 4464 *Bittern* has a northbound express in the Thirsk area (around halfway between the two places) during the late 1930s. The locomotive was new to Heaton shed, north east of Newcastle, in mid-December 1937 and remained the sole member of the class there for several years, later departing in March 1943. Heaton was mainly the home of the area's freight locomotives, although there were some passenger duties and the A4 was generally used on the early morning Newcastle to King's Cross train, with crews lodging overnight before returning northward with the 'Flying Scotsman'. Photograph courtesy Rail Photoprints.

*Opposite page* NO. 4464 – KING'S CROSS STATION

No. 4464 *Bittern* departs from King's Cross station in late February 1939 with the 'Flying Scotsman' service to Edinburgh Waverley. This train had been the most famous on the East Coast Main Line from the 1860s and traditionally left London at 10.00, taking 8 hours 30 minutes for much of the early 20th century. The LNER worked hard to exploit the prestige of the 'Flying Scotsman' and managed to make the train the world's longest distance non-stop express in 1928. This was followed in the early 1930s by reductions in timings and the journey of 392 miles was completed in just over seven hours. Whilst the non-stop only ran in the summer months and had a restricted formation, the train travelled with two extra coaches for the rest of the year and portions were destined for other places, such as Glasgow and Perth, whereas the non-stop only served Edinburgh and Aberdeen. No. 4464 was restricted to only being able to work the winter 'Flying Scotsman' as the engine was fitted with a streamlined non-corridor tender, unlike other classmates that had the connection.

Although the East Coast route had served the far north east of Scotland from the late 19th century, the LNER was the first company to promote the train with a name – the 'Aberdonian' – from 1927. The service traditionally departed from King's Cross around 19.35 and was scheduled to take 12 hours to reach Aberdeen. Whilst slow by the standards reached in the late 1930s, the train was particularly heavy, with portions for several places in the north of Scotland during both the summer and winter months. The line between Edinburgh and Aberdeen was also particularly formidable, possessing difficult gradients, which induced Gresley to design the P2 Class 2-8-2s for work on the route with the Aberdeen sleeper train. In part due to the popularity of the A4 Class, the P2s were modified in the late 1930s to use the streamlined front end design. No. 4465 *Guillemot* is in charge of a northbound 'Aberdonian' train at Brookmans Park during 1938.

*Opposite below* NO. 4465 – KING'S CROSS STATION
A footplateman climbs into the cab of no. 4465 *Guillemot* as the engine stands at the head of an express soon to depart from King's Cross station, around 1938. The station's signalbox is in the background (at the end of platforms 5/6) and was of relatively recent construction, dating from 1932 when replacing two old Great Northern Railway boxes; one – West box – was immediately to the left of the new box as viewed here. The LNER had instigated a major resignalling project at King's Cross during the early 1930s, as an all-electric system with colour light signals was adopted in place of the old equipment, which required frequent and time consuming maintenance. Interestingly, much of the wiring was carried to the signal box on the gantry seen above the locomotive, but had to be removed and rerouted in the late 1940s following a mishap with A4 no. 2512 *Silver Fox*.

*Below* NO. 4465
No. 4465 *Guillemot* is working an express at an unidentified location during the late 1930s. Constructed at Doncaster Works in January 1938, the locomotive was allocated to Gateshead.

NO. 4466 – GRANTHAM SHED

No. 4466 *Herring Gull* enjoyed the glamour of King's Cross shed for only three months from new in early 1938, even working on the streamlined expresses. In late April the locomotive was one of two A4s – the other being no. 4494 *Osprey* – dispatched to Grantham for use on the northbound 'Aberdonian' as far as Edinburgh. The crew would then lodge to return the following night with an Anglo-Scottish express. No. 4466 is on a servicing pit at Grantham shed, with the station visible to the right.

*Above* NO. 4466 – DONCASTER WORKS

No. 4466 became the second A4 to carry the name *Sir Ralph Wedgwood* following the destruction of no. 4469 at York during an air raid in 1942. No. 4466 was not renamed until January 1944 and has been photographed to mark the change at Doncaster Works.

*Below* No. 4466 – RETFORD STATION

A southbound express has paused at Retford station in the late 1930s, with no. 4466 *Herring Gull* leading.

*Opposite above* NO. 4467 – WELWYN GARDEN CITY
No. 4467 *Wild Swan* was the final A4 to enter service with only the number applied at the front end. From the following engine, no. 4468, 'Class A4' was also present underneath. No. 4467 is coupled to an express that is rushing southward past Welwyn Garden City on 8th April 1939. Built some 14 months earlier, the additional text at buffer level was likely added at the engine's general repair, which was completed at Doncaster in late February 1939.

*Opposite below* NO. 4467 – DONCASTER STATION
No. 4467 *Wild Swan* has a northbound express at Doncaster station during 1938. At this time, the locomotive was King's Cross-allocated and was there until May 1939 when transferred to Doncaster. The engine was one of four A4s allocated to the depot for a period at the end of the 1930s and into the early 1940s, with the others being no. 4468 *Mallard*, no. 4900 *Gannet* and no. 4903 *Peregrine*.

*Below* NO. 4467 – KING'S CROSS STATION
A luxury service offered by the LNER throughout the 1930s was the 'Northern Belle' tourist train, which ran in June. Passengers departed from King's Cross on Friday evening and were conveyed through the night to a place of interest in the north of England. From there, they visited other parts of the North and Scotland, before returning to London on Thursday evening. Accommodation, meals and other methods of travel were covered as part of the 'Northern Belle' service and the tours were particularly popular, if expensive. A Pacific usually worked the train on the main line and here no. 4467 *Wild Swan* has the honour of leading one of the 1938 tours out of King's Cross.

*Opposite above* NO. 4468 – KING'S CROSS STATION

New in March 1938, no. 4468 *Mallard*, which is arriving at King's Cross station with an express, was the first A4 locomotive to carry the class designation under the number from new. A front access panel to reach oiling apparatus was also omitted when the engine was completed. Yet, the distinguishing feature of great note for no. 4468 was the first fitting of a Kylchap double chimney and blastpipe to an A4. This arrangement had been developed from the design of André Chapelon of the Paris-Orleans Railway in France and had been first used by Gresley on P2 Class 2-8-2 no. 2001 *Cock o' the North* from new. The apparatus served to improve the draught through the boiler and reduce back pressure in the cylinders to create greater efficiency. Gresley had also used the double chimney and blastpipe with his W1 Class locomotive, as well as A3 Pacific no. 2751 *Humorist* and was satisfied that a good improvement on normal operation was achievable. The design of the Kylchap exhaust fitted to no. 4468 *Mallard* was similar to that used by no. 2751 rather than the P2, with a smaller orifice at 5 in. diameter.

*Opposite below* NO. 4468 – KING'S CROSS STATION

When quite new, no. 4468 *Mallard* has been pictured in King's Cross station's servicing yard. This was located on the west side of the site on a relatively narrow strip of land and was required due to the volume of traffic restricting the movements to and from the shed, which was a relatively short distance away. King's Cross Suburban station is on the left.

*Below* NO. 4468 – KING'S CROSS STATION

No. 4468 *Mallard* was based at Doncaster from entering traffic, likely for the works to keep updated on the running of the engine, due to the use of the Kylchap chimney arrangement. The engine was in the 'top link' at the shed and this included Driver Duddington and Fireman Bray; both are seen here on the footplate, as the engine waits to depart with the 17.50 to Leeds on 17th June 1938. The same crew was in charge of *Mallard* some two weeks later when the locomotive achieved the speed record for steam traction with 125 mph recorded near Little Bytham between Grantham and Peterborough.

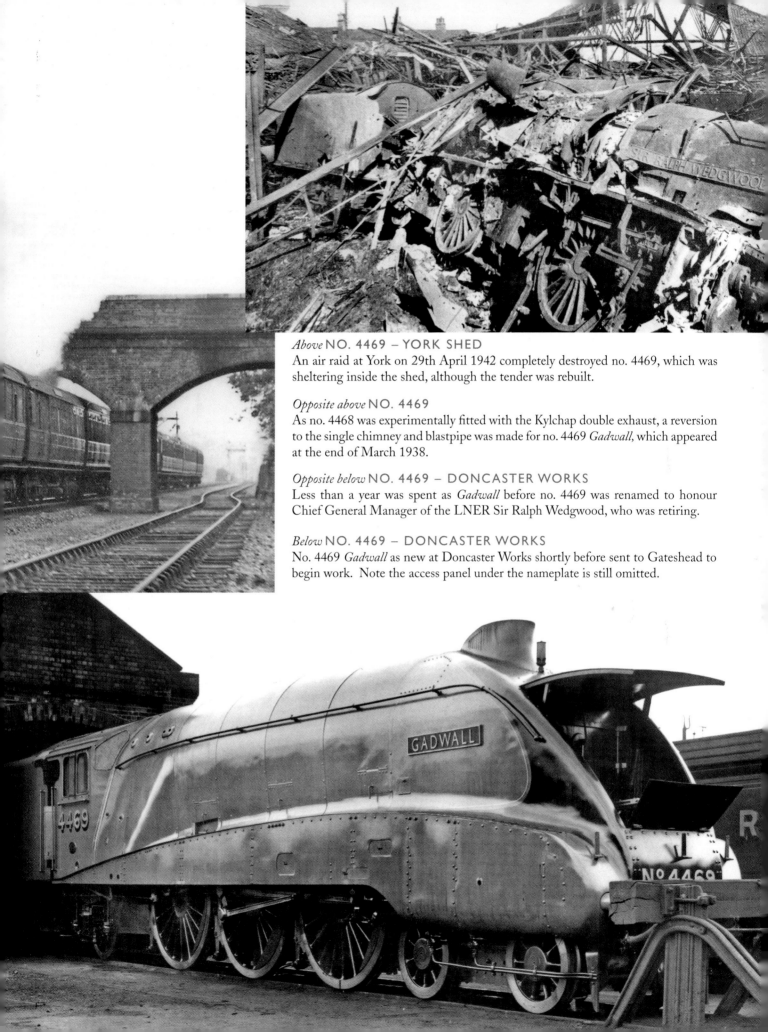

*Above* NO. 4469 – YORK SHED

An air raid at York on 29th April 1942 completely destroyed no. 4469, which was sheltering inside the shed, although the tender was rebuilt.

*Opposite above* NO. 4469

As no. 4468 was experimentally fitted with the Kylchap double exhaust, a reversion to the single chimney and blastpipe was made for no. 4469 *Gadwall*, which appeared at the end of March 1938.

*Opposite below* NO. 4469 – DONCASTER WORKS

Less than a year was spent as *Gadwall* before no. 4469 was renamed to honour Chief General Manager of the LNER Sir Ralph Wedgwood, who was retiring.

*Below* NO. 4469 – DONCASTER WORKS

No. 4469 *Gadwall* as new at Doncaster Works shortly before sent to Gateshead to begin work. Note the access panel under the nameplate is still omitted.

*Opposite above* NO. 4499 – KING'S CROSS STATION
A midday express begins the journey away from King's Cross station, with no. 4499 *Pochard* leading the train towards Gas Works Tunnel on 8th January 1939. Built at Doncaster in April 1938, the locomotive was Gateshead-allocated from this time and was soon to be renamed after the Deputy Chairman of the LNER Sir Murrough Wilson.

*Opposite below* NO. 4499
During no. 4499 *Pochard's* first year in service, the engine has been caught at an unidentified location with an express. The locomotive was the first A4 to be sent into traffic with a hinged access plate below the name, although this is the early two-hinge version and would later be changed to use three hinges.

*Below* NO. 4499 – GRANTHAM
On the turntable at Grantham is no. 4499 which has the nameplates covered. The engine was officially named *Sir Murrough Wilson* from April 1939. Perhaps thanks to this change, no. 4499 had the honour of working one of the final 'Silver Jubilee' services before the outbreak of war – the other was headed by no. 4489 *Dominion of Canada*. Also as a result of the naming, the locomotive switched from shaded transfer numbers and letters to the metal versions, whilst the opening under the name is now the three-hinge type.

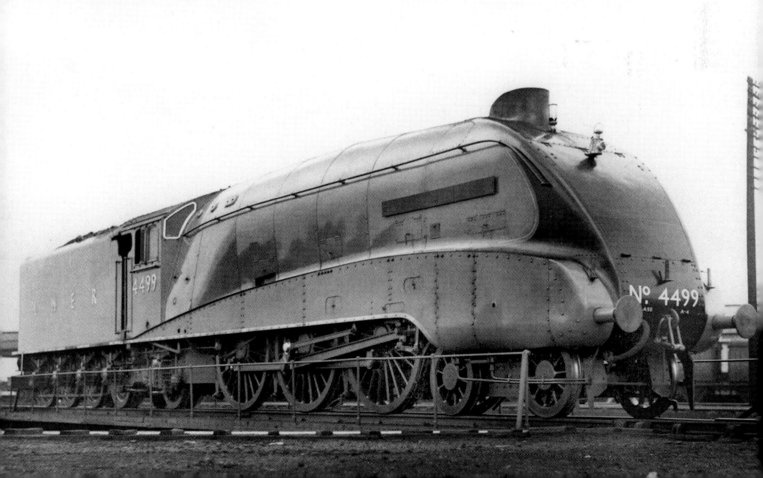

*Above* NO. 4500 – DONCASTER WORKS

By the end of the 1930s, a trend to rename members of the A4 Class had begun. No. 4500 was one engine to be ensnared in this practice and after carrying *Garganey* from April 1938, the locomotive became known as *Sir Ronald Matthews* in honour of William Whitelaw's successor as the LNER's Chairman. No. 4500 also received metal numbering and lettering at the changeover, which occurred in March 1939; the engine is at Doncaster Works at this time.

*Opposite above* NO. 4500 – SANDY

Forty-four miles north of King's Cross and between Hitchin and Huntingdon, no. 4500 *Sir Ronald Matthews* speeds past Sandy with an express from Edinburgh Waverley to the capital on 28th August 1939. No. 4500 was allocated from new to Gateshead shed and, interestingly, was the only A4 – apart from no. 4469 *Gadwall/Sir Ralph Wedgwood* – to spend their career at one depot. Nos 4499 and 4500 filled in two vacant numbers between A4 no. 4498 *Sir Nigel Gresley* and no. 4501, the first locomotive of H.A. Ivatt's Great Northern Railway C2 (LNER C12) 4-4-2T Class introduced in 1898.

*Opposite below* NO. 4500 – GRANTHAM STATION

The first station in Grantham was built in 1850 by the Ambergate, Nottingham, Boston & Eastern Junction Railway and located on a site to the north west of the town. The Great Northern Railway did not arrive until 1852, with the completion of the line from Peterborough to Retford. Grantham station was designed by Henry Goddard, who had a practice in Lincoln and produced the other stations on the section. Construction was carried out by Kirk & Parry of Sleaford. The station was later modified by the LNER in the late 1930s, as work took place to improve the platforms and canopies. No. 4500 *Sir Ronald Matthews* is between duties at Grantham during this period.

## *Below* NO. 4900 – DONCASTER SHED

No. 4900 *Gannet* devours the attention of a group of female cleaners at Doncaster shed during the early 1940s. Following the outbreak of war, a certain amount of the LNER's staff left to take positions with the armed forces and over the course of the conflict some 24,500 men and 1,000 women departed from the company. This left a substantial gap in the workforce and around 15,000 women were drafted in to take up the slack. Yet, there was a problem in recruitment in general, and the railways failed to offer attractive employment opportunities, as might be demonstrated with this image. Although cleaning a grimy locomotive might be 'heavenly' for some railway enthusiasts, for the majority such a prospect was unthinkable. Other avenues of employment in wartime industries, such as munitions and aircraft manufacture, offered much better rates of pay and further contributed on the drain of manpower away from the railways.

*Above* NO. 4900 – THIRSK

No. 4900 *Gannet* approaches Thirsk station with a southbound 'Flying Scotsman' service in 1939. The locomotive is probably working the train early in the year whilst still allocated to King's Cross; this stay lasted from September 1938 to May 1939 when transferred to Doncaster. The engine had been new to the latter depot in May 1938 and was briefly at Grantham before moving to 'top shed'. No. 4900 was also only equipped with a streamlined non-corridor tender which rules out the non-stop 'Flying Scotsman'. *Gannet* appears to have been used at least once on either the 'Silver Jubilee' or the 'West Riding Limited' as only one A4 is recorded to have not worked one of the high-speed expresses.

Gresley was evidently pleased with the performance of no. 4468 *Mallard*, as the continuation of the original authority to fit four A4s with Kylchap double blastpipes and chimneys was approved. No. 4901 *Capercaillie* was the first of the final three class members to be fitted with the apparatus when entering service in June 1938. Allocated to Gateshead, the locomotive has a northbound express at York in the late 1930s.

Whilst Sir Nigel Gresley was the only employee of the LNER to be honoured with his name on an A4 when the locomotive was new, several officials subsequently enjoyed a similar tribute. The successor to Sir Ralph Wedgwood as Chief General Manager was Charles H. Newton and his name adorned no. 4901 from August 1942, although the plates had to be amended during the following year after he received a knighthood. No. 4901 has undergone the first alteration here at Doncaster Works, with the removal of the skirting and change to black livery with 'NE' lettering also occurring at this time.

No. 4901 *Capercaillie* sails through Doncaster station with a southbound express in the late 1930s.

*Opposite above* NO. 4902 – DONCASTER STATION

No. 4902 *Seagull* passes through Doncaster station with a southbound express in the late 1930s. Even though the A4s were particularly known during the late 1930s for working the high-speed expresses, which were short and light trains for the time, the class was equally able when long and heavy trains were coupled behind, such as this one. A record of *Seagull*'s performance with a relatively heavy train appears in O.S. Nock's *The Gresley Pacifics 1935-1974* to demonstrate this haulage capability. The engine had a train weighing 590 tons leaving King's Cross but was hampered by several signals north of the capital. No. 4902 was subsequently able to average 67 mph between Hitchin and Huntingdon and reach 70 mph at the top of Stoke Summit. The first stop was made at Grantham under the schedule and with delays factored in could have drastically reduced the time.

*Opposite below* NO. 4902

No. 4902 *Seagull* has an express at an unidentified location at the end of the 1930s.

*Below* NO. 4902 – DONCASTER WORKS

No. 4902 *Seagull* is at Doncaster Works in the late 1930s. Rather than being pictured when new in late June 1938, the engine appears to be slightly service worn and no. 4902 could have been caught during a light repair that was carried out in early September. *Seagull* was in traffic for around 15 months before the first general repair was carried out and not until the third general ended in May 1942 was the skirting removed and black livery applied.

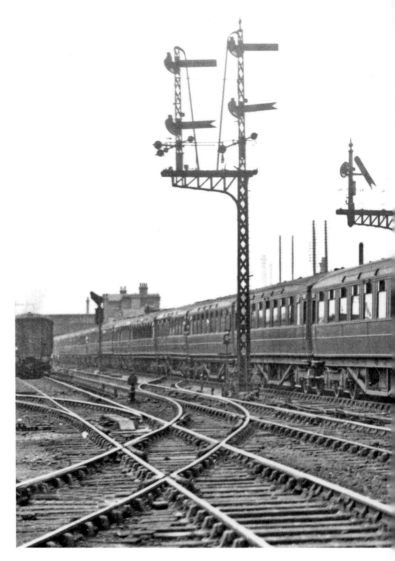

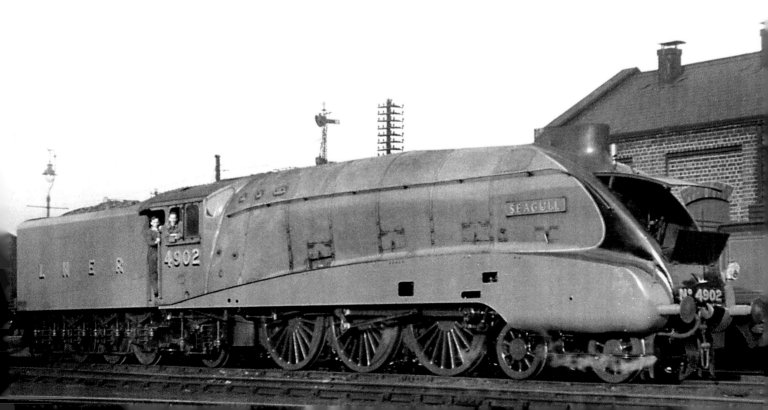

*Above* NO. 4903 – NEW SOUTHGATE

On 10th September 1938, no. 4903 *Peregrine* leads the 16.00 express to Leeds through New Southgate. The locomotive was the last of the A4 class in service, although there were plans to further develop the design before Gresley's death in 1941. Even after the Second World War, the last Chief Mechanical Engineer of the LNER, A.H. Peppercorn, briefly considered continuing the shape of the A4 front end for his A1 Class Pacifics introduced in 1948.

*Above* NO. 4903 – DONCASTER SHED

No. 4903 *Peregrine* was officially completed on 1st July 1938 and the engine stands here at Doncaster shed on the 2nd, which was a Saturday. The locomotive would perhaps begin work from the depot on Monday, following classmate no. 4468 *Mallard*'s record-breaking run.

*Below* NO. 4903 – KING'S CROSS SHED

When no. 4903 *Peregrine* entered traffic, King's Cross shed held the highest number of A4s with 11 class members. Many others would have daily visitors on trains from the north, such as Doncaster's no. 4903 which is on the turntable at King's Cross shed, likely in the summer of 1939, as the front access panel in front of the cylinders is now fitted.

*Above* NO. 1

As mentioned earlier in this book, the locomotive numbering system adopted by the majority of the LNER's constituents was relatively haphazard and tended to fill gaps between classes, or spaces left by withdrawn locomotives. The LNER followed similar lines after Grouping, perhaps due to the size of the task of reorganising the numbers of approx. 7,000 locomotives inherited. Such a project was not contemplated until Gresley's successor Edward Thompson took office and published a plan for the wholesale change of the numbering scheme in 1943. In essence, this gave several classes of locomotive, i.e. express passenger, freight, etc, blocks of 1,000 numbers. The A4s with the names of prominent officers of the LNER were given the first four numbers before a large gap was left – for Thompson's own Pacifics yet to be built – then Gresley's A1s and A3s took 500-578, before the remaining A4s carried 580 to 613, with gaps left for those taking 1-4. Owing to the Second World War, the scheme was held in abeyance until the end of hostilities. The renumbering was finally taken up in early 1946 and four A4s received new numbers before a halt was called for a recasting of the scheme. All of the A4s were moved to the head of the list and occupied numbers 1-34. No thought was given to arranging the locomotives in construction order and those named after important personages were given precedence. The new numbers were subsequently applied to the A4s between May 1946 and January 1947. Here, no. 1 *Sir Ronald Matthews* has an express around 1947.

*Below* NO. 1
No. 4500 became no. 1 in mid-November 1946 following a general repair at Doncaster Works. At this time, the locomotive also returned to Garter Blue livery, after five years in wartime black. No. 1 *Sir Ronald Matthews* stands on an unidentified turntable with the 'Flying Scotsman' headboard around 1947.

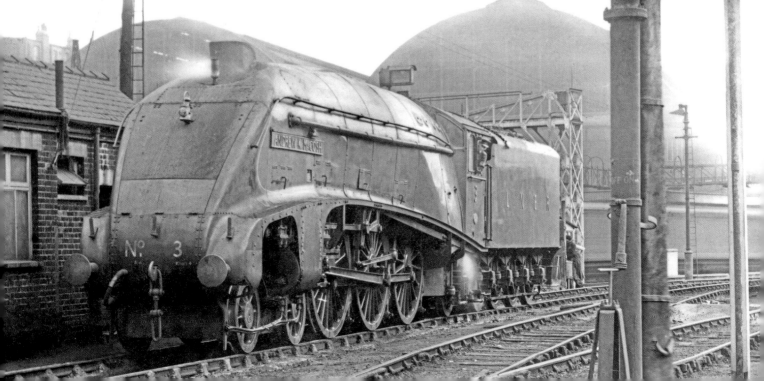

*Opposite above* NO. 6 – NEW SOUTHGATE

No. 4466 *Sir Ralph Wedgwood* was one of the four A4s to display the originally allocated number in the 1943 scheme, which for the locomotive was no. 605. The engine received this at King's Cross shed in late January 1946 and ran until May 1946 before the newly allocated no. 6 was applied. *Sir Ralph Wedgwood* has a northbound express at New Southgate.

*Opposite below* NO. 3 – KING'S CROSS STATION

No. 3 *Andrew K. McCosh* poses in the locomotive yard at King's Cross station. The engine had been no. 4494 until September 1946 when renumbered at home shed King's Cross, which is acknowledged at buffer level here with 'King's +'. No. 3 was still in black livery at this time and would not return to Garter Blue until June 1947.

*Below* NO. 3

At an unidentified location, no. 3 *Andrew K. McCosh* has an express around 1948. Tender changes were relatively infrequent for the A4 Class, yet no. 3 had a brief change in late 1945 taking tender no. 5584 from Gresley A3 no. 2563 *Tagalie* which was in Doncaster Works at the time. This was of the streamlined non-corridor type and replaced corridor tender no. 5649 that evidently required attention. No. 3 went on to have several other changes during the 1950s.

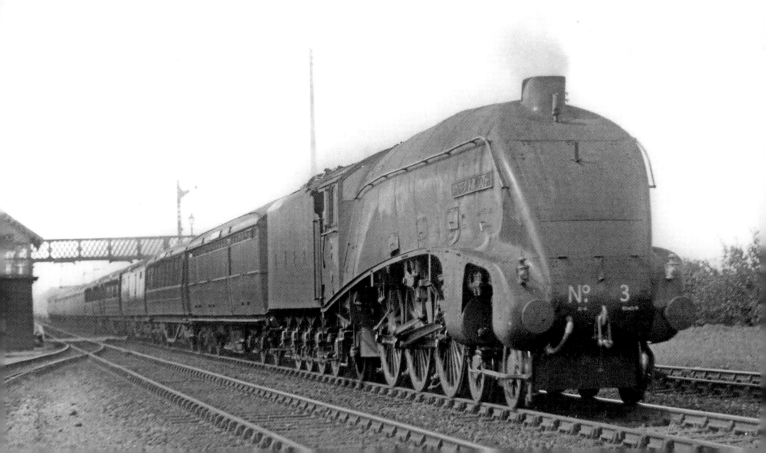

*Above* NO. 8 – POTTERS BAR

The LNER hoped that General Eisenhower would come to England to christen no. 4496 and the plates were covered for a time following naming in September 1945. Yet, his duties over this period made such an event impossible and the nameplates were uncovered without any ceremony. This was done before the engine was renumbered 8 in late November 1946 during a general repair. No. 8 *Dwight D. Eisenhower* had been the first A4 to return to Garter Blue livery after the war as part of the previous general repair. The locomotive has a southbound freight train at Potters Bar around 1948.

*Opposite above* NO. 10 – DONCASTER STATION

A particularly grimy no. 10 *Dominion of Canada* heads away from Doncaster station with a northbound express around 1947/1948. The locomotive had discarded no. 4489 in May 1946 but did not return to Garter Blue until November 1947. Despite the wartime conditions, the engine managed to retain the bell, though not operational. This change had occurred pre-war following a mishap where the bell was rung for a young enthusiast at King's Cross, only to malfunction and continue to York, where the engine had to be replaced. No. 10 had a corridor tender from new and the porthole-style window is visible here. The tender is no. 5328, which was taken from no. 4490 *Empire of India* in December 1937, replacing no. 5326 built with the engine and taken subsequently by the latter. No. 10 is passing the new and old Doncaster North signal boxes. The new box was the result of a modernisation programme started just before the war and not completed until the end of the 1940s.

*Opposite below* NO. 11 – NEWCASTLE STATION

A late afternoon express to Glasgow leaves Newcastle station behind no. 11 *Empire of India* in 1947. The locomotive had recently returned to Garter Blue livery at a general repair in November 1946, at which point no. 4490 became no. 11. A further change carried out whilst at Doncaster was the increase in cut-off from 65% to 75%. This allowed the A4s more power when starting with heavy trains, which were particularly prevalent at the time. All of Gresley's three cylinder engines were limited in this way and had been from the early 1920s, following an instance of the valve over travelling and hitting the valve cover during a test.

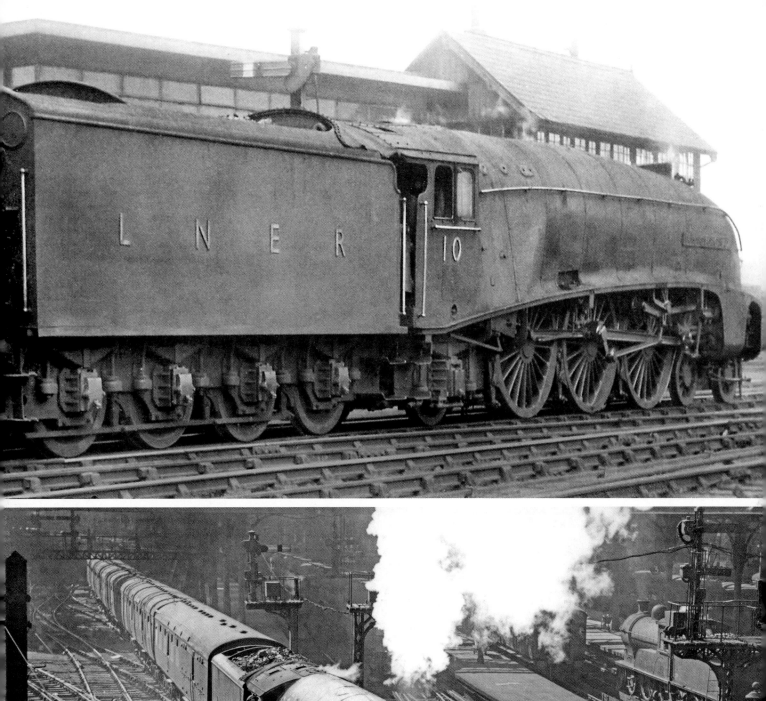

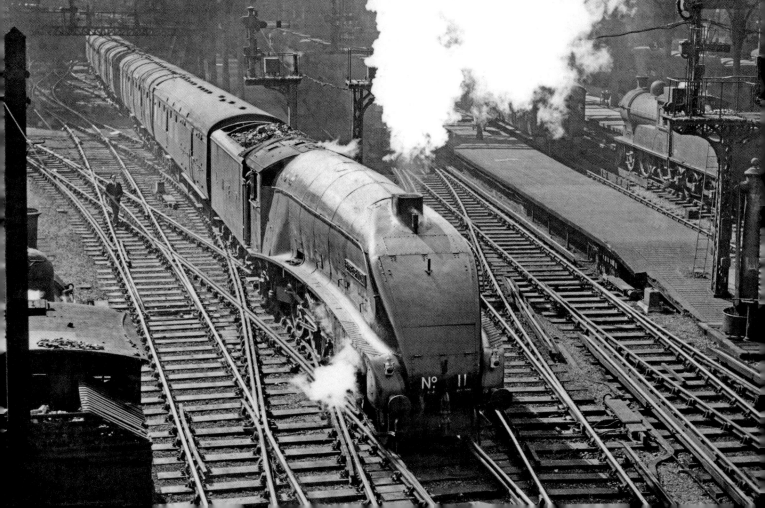

*Above* NO. 11 – NEWCASTLE STATION

No. 11 *Empire of India* stands with an express at Newcastle station during August 1947.  Photograph courtesy Colour-Rail.

*Below* NO. 12 – NEWCASTLE STATION

No. 12 *Commonwealth of Australia* is at the head of the 'Flying Scotsman' at Newcastle station in 1947.

*Above* NO. 14 – DONCASTER WORKS

Fresh from a general repair at Doncaster Works in August 1947 is no. 14 *Silver Link*. The engine was the first A4 to emerge with the 1946 numbering and Garter Blue livery, which was specially carried out for an exhibition in Edinburgh. Photograph by Doug Brown.

*Below* NO. 14 – GANWICK

*Silver Link* had a few weeks left as no. 14 when captured at Ganwick on 18th April 1949. The locomotive soon underwent a general repair and took the BR number. Note the metal 'R' on the tender appears to have been lost, perhaps on this Edinburgh train's journey from Grantham to King's Cross.

NO. 16 – DONCASTER
Just south of Doncaster station, no. 16 *Silver King* heads the 'Flying Scotsman' express on 17th June 1947.

*Above and Below* NO. 16 - BARKSTON

This set of photographs was captured on 9th May 1947, after no. 16 *Silver King* had travelled from Doncaster Works to Barkston (just north of Grantham) for running-in following a general repair. Barkston was the primary destination for this task and no. 16 was accompanied (below) by Thompson A2/3 Class Pacific no. 521 *Watling Street*. The driver of no. 16 was Fred Sleaford (seen left and right in the cab of the engine) and the young man oiling the trailing axle is John Mayne; the other gentleman is unfortunately unidentified. All photographs by Doug Brown.

*Above* NO. 21 – KING'S CROSS

No. 21 *Wild Swan* has burst out of Gas Works Tunnel, just north of King's Cross station, with a northbound express in 1947. At 528 yards long, and featuring a gradient of 1 in 107, the tunnel could pose a challenge for locomotives with heavy trains leaving the station, especially during the war.

*Opposite above* NO. 17 – FINSBURY PARK

A quite dirty no. 17 *Silver Fox* has been dispatched to Hornsey Carriage Sidings for a relatively short train around 1947. The engine is returning to King's Cross station through Finsbury Park, being just north of the station. *Silver Fox* was renumbered in September 1946 and returned to Garter Blue livery in September 1947.

*Opposite below* NO. 22 – READING

Pre-Nationalisation, there was little chance of an A4 leaving the confines of the LNER's territory. The formation of British Railways resulted in an evaluation of the inherited classes in preparation for the introduction of Standard Classes. This saw engines travel across the country to determine the suitability of their characteristics in foreign areas. Here, no. 22 *Mallard* is in the Western Region at Reading with an express bound for Plymouth during the 1948 exchange trials.

*Opposite above* NO. E22 – MARSHMOOR

Planning for the formation of British Railways on 1st January 1948 did not stretch to devising a numbering scheme that would encompass all the absorbed locomotives. An early system adopted in the former LNER territories was an 'E' prefix, although few engines were changed and this was discontinued by mid-1948. Just four A4s received the 'E', with no. 22 *Mallard* being changed in March 1948. The prefix could be located either above or in front of the number of the bufferbeam and the same was true of the cabside number. *Mallard* initially only had the prefix above the cab number, though this was later applied above buffer level. The locomotive has the northbound 'Yorkshire Pullman' service at Marshmoor on 19th April 1949.

*Opposite below* NO. 25

The war years took a terrible toll on Britain's railways due to the volume of traffic and lack of maintenance. In 1946 an attempt was made to improve passenger services, which had been restricted in favour of freight movement. The track and permanent way was in such an advanced state of disrepair that in 1947 a reduction of services was necessary for works to be carried out. A speed limit of 75 mph was also in force for a number of years after the end of the war. The 'Flying Scotsman' continued throughout the conflict, although the non-stop was not reintroduced until 1948. No. 25 *Falcon* has the express here at an unidentified location during the late 1940s.

*Below* NO. 25

No. 25 *Falcon* was at King's Cross shed for much of the 1940s, though between April 1948 and March 1950 the locomotive worked from Grantham. *Falcon* became no. 25 in May 1946 and at the same time received Garter Blue livery, along with metal numbers and lettering.

*Above* NO. 28 – DONCASTER WORKS

The renaming of A4s did not stop with no. 8 *Dwight D. Eisenhower,* as the prospect of the formation of British Railways induced the LNER to further recognise servants of the company. One such person was Walter K. Whigham, who became Deputy Chairman upon the death of Sir Murrough Wilson in 1946. No. 4487 *Sea Eagle*, which was renumbered 28 in November 1946, was chosen and took the new name in late 1947. The engine returned to Garter Blue at this time and also received metal numbers and letters. A new addition, which is visible on the cab side, is the Route Availability number. Simply, this scheme restricted the sphere of operation for various classes based on the axle load using a scale from 1-9, with the high number denoting the widest limitation. The A4 Class had R.A. 9, along with the other Pacifics and V2s, and this was applied on the cab side – sometimes in various positions – with 2 in. high yellow lettering.

*Opposite Page* NO. 27 – DONCASTER WORKS

In January 1947, Doncaster Works photographer Ben Burrell entered the Paint Shop and captured this scene which was then sent to artist Terence Cuneo, who had been commissioned to produce a painting for advertising purposes. This later found fame as the 'Giants Refreshed' poster. No. 27 *Merlin* receives the finishing touches to the restored Garter Blue livery from Doug Monday (left) and Jack Ellis (right), whilst new Thompson A2/3 Class Pacific no. 519 *Honeyway* has the nameplates fitted; note classmate of the latter's no. 520 *Owen Tudor*'s nameplate is on the bench to the left. A certain amount of 'artistic licence' has been taken, as in the finished painting no. 27 has transformed into no. 1 *Sir Ronald Matthews* and the A2/3 has also changed to no. 520 *Owen Tudor*. Interestingly, both of the engines in the original picture became shedmates at Edinburgh Haymarket when they entered traffic later in the month.

*Above* NO. 29 – NEW SOUTHGATE

No. 29 *Woodcock* has a Newcastle-bound express at New Southgate around 1948. At the reintroduction of the Garter Blue livery, the decision was made to provide cut out metal numbers and lettering for all members of the class, rather than specially selected engines. No. 29 lost the black livery in July 1947 and at this time reverted to the chime whistle, which appears to be in use here, following the fitting of a bell-shape standard whistle during the war. The sound of the chime whistle was thought to be similar enough to an air-raid siren for them to be removed from almost all of the class.

*Opposite above* NO. 30 – NEW SOUTHGATE

To continue with the change of whistle mentioned above, no. 30 *Golden Fleece* has the LNER standard bell-shape whistle fitted here, but would revert to the chime type during 1948. The locomotive has the local King's Cross to Cambridge train at New Southgate on 6th October 1947. No. 30 was allocated to Grantham at this time, arriving from King's Cross in July 1942 and remaining until June 1950, when returning to the capital.

*Opposite below* NO. 32 – GREENWOOD

Another Grantham engine is leaving the capital with a northbound express. In this instance the A4 is no. 32 *Gannet*, which was allocated there over a similar period to no. 30, but arrived a year later from Doncaster.

NO. 60001 – GATESHEAD SHED
At Gateshead shed c. 1960 is no. 60001 *Sir
Ronald Matthews*. Photograph by Bill Reed.

*Above* NO. 60001 – DONCASTER WORKS

An interesting image of no. 60001 *Sir Ronald Matthews* completely stripped in Doncaster Works Crimpsall Repair Shop on 17th September 1961. The locomotive is in the midst of the final general repair, which would keep no. 60001 in service for another three years. Photograph by Cedric Clayson courtesy John Clayson.

*Below* NO. 60001 – LEEDS NEVILLE HILL

On 29th April 1962 no. 60001 *Sir Ronald Matthews* has an express at Neville Hill, Leeds. Photograph courtesy Colour-Rail.

NO. 60001 – STOKE SUMMIT
In the late 1950s, no. 60001 *Sir Ronald Matthews* has an express at Stoke Summit. Photograph courtesy Rail Photoprints.

*Above* NO. 60001 – PETERBOROUGH STATION

No. 60001 *Sir Ronald Matthews* has an express at Peterborough station on 7th July 1960. Photograph courtesy Colour-Rail.

*Below* NO. 60001

At an unidentified location, no. 60001 *Sir Ronald Matthews* is at the head of a King's Cross to Glasgow express on 3rd June 1956. The engine would upgrade to the Kylchap exhaust system in two years' time. Photograph courtesy Colour-Rail.

*Opposite above* NO. 60002 – GRANTHAM STATION

Whilst the A4 Class was primarily devoted to express passenger trains, King's Cross, Edinburgh Haymarket and Gateshead depots had A4s rostered to work freight trains throughout the lifetime of the class. The most famous of these was mid-afternoon fully fitted freight (with wagons vacuum braked throughout) from King's Cross to Edinburgh, or 'Scotch Goods', which was invariably hauled by an A4. No. 60002 *Sir Murrough Wilson* is likely at the head of this train at Grantham station on 31st August 1961. Photograph by Cedric Clayson courtesy John Clayson.

*Opposite below* NO. 60002 – YORK SHED

Around six weeks in service remained for no. 60002 *Sir Murrough Wilson* when caught at York shed on 23rd March 1964. The engine had been Gateshead-allocated from new in April 1938, apart from two months at King's Cross in 1943. No. 60002 is in the shed yard with A3 Class Pacific no. 60112 *St Simon*, which was based at Peterborough at this time and withdrawn by the end of the year. Photograph courtesy Colour-Rail.

*Below* NO. 60002 – PERTH

No. 60002 *Sir Murrough Wilson* has travelled a fair distance away from home at Gateshead c. 1960 and has reached Perth with a train. The locomotive was paired with streamlined non-corridor tender no. 5673 from new until condemned. This type was used with the last 14 class members, ten of which received new tenders, whilst the remaining four had reconditioned examples taken from the A3 Class. Apart from the lack of a corridor, there were only a few detail differences between the two types of tender. Photograph by Bill Reed.

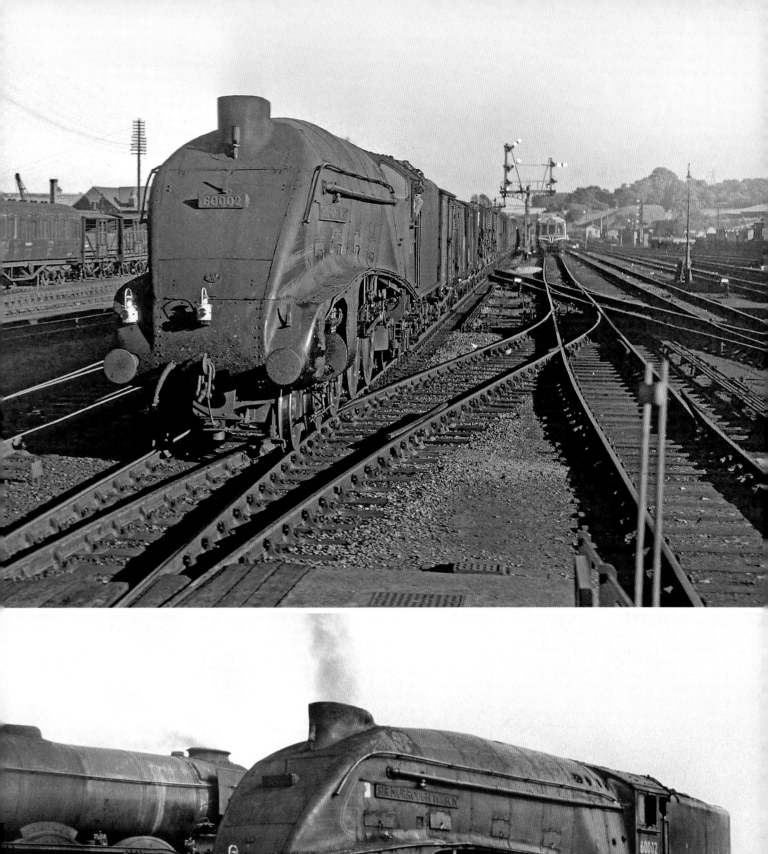

*Opposite above* NO. 60002 – SUNDERLAND

View south from Forfar Street, Sunderland, as A4 no. 60002 *Sir Murrough Wilson* approaches with a loaded ballast train on 17th May 1962. This is quite an unusual working for the locomotive, as is the absence of the dome cover and the covers for the wash-out plugs. Perhaps maintenance has been carried out and the engine is being run in before fully returning to traffic. No. 60002's last general repair was carried out in January 1961, leaving the engine in service for the next three years without works attention. The locomotive did have a fresh boiler fitted at this time, no. 29320, which previously had been with no. 60006 *Sir Ralph Wedgwood*. Photograph by D.J. Dippie.

*Opposite below* NO. 60002 – ST NEOTS

Fifty-two miles from King's Cross station at St Neots, no. 60002 *Sir Murrough Wilson* leads the 'Flying Scotsman' southward on 12th October 1961. Photograph courtesy Colour-Rail.

*Below* NO. 60002 – NEWCASTLE STATION

Ready to journey southward with a late afternoon express at Newcastle station on 1st August 1960 is no. 60002 *Sir Murrough Wilson*. Photograph by D.J. Dippie.

**Opposite above** NO. 60003 – GRANTHAM STATION

Shortly after Nationalisation, BR announced the introduction of a new high-speed service between King's Cross and Newcastle. LNER enthusiasts would have been disappointed to learn this was not the 'Silver Jubilee', which did not ultimately reappear, rather a new Pullman service named the 'Tees-Tyne Pullman'. The train first ran on 27th September 1948 with similar departure times to the 'Silver Jubilee', but with another hour on the schedule and consequently slower average speed. The 'Tees-Tyne Pullman' subsequently ran until the end of steam on the East Coast Main Line – not being completely discontinued until 1976. No. 60003 *Andrew K. McCosh* has a northbound train here at Grantham on 31st August 1961. Photograph by Cedric Clayson courtesy John Clayson.

**Opposite below** NO. 60003 – DARLINGTON STATION

The railways first arrived at Darlington in 1829 with the opening of the pioneer Stockton & Darlington Railway. The town later saw the Newcastle to York main line pass through, with a restrictive flat crossing over the busy S&D route, and Darlington became a major transfer point. The station opened on the main line was originally quite small and had to be expanded in the 1860s, then again in the 1880s. The new station was completed in 1887 to the designs of noted architect William Bell. A three-span roof covered, in essence, a large island platform with bays central at either end. A southbound train is at the eastern side of Darlington station on 17th August 1961, with no. 60003 *Andrew K. McCosh* admired by the local enthusiasts. Photograph courtesy Colour-Rail.

**Below** NO. 60003 – GAINSBOROUGH

No. 60003 *Andrew K. McCosh* appears to have been diverted off the main line with this express and has been caught at Gainsborough during the early 1960s. Photograph courtesy Colour-Rail.

*Opposite above* NO. 60003 – DONCASTER STATION

In the early 1950s, BR fitted several A4s with experimental apparatus in the cab which warned crews of adverse signals. No. 60003 *Andrew K. McCosh* was a recipient in April 1950 and the mounting plate is visible here between the bogie wheels under the drawhook. The locomotive is at the north end of Doncaster station (viewed from the Cattle Dock) on 23rd March 1952 with a southbound express. Photograph by Geoff Warnes.

*Opposite below* NO. 60003 – MONKWEARMOUTH

No. 60003 *Andrew K. McCosh* has a midday express just north of Sunderland at Monkwearmouth on 6th June 1962. Apart from short spells at Grantham in 1941 and 1957, the locomotive was a long-term resident of King's Cross depot. BR Class 03 diesel shunter no. D2065 is on the left. Photograph by D.J. Dippie.

*Below* NO. 60003 – GRANTHAM STATION

The driver of no. 60003 *Andrew K. McCosh* watches for the guard's signal before departing with a northbound express at Grantham on 24th May 1962. The wiring from the AWS equipment fitted under the bufferbeam can be seen attached to the side of the running plate, along with the lines from the speed indicator coupled to the rear driving wheel. Photograph by Cedric Clayson courtesy John Clayson.

*Above* NO. 60004 GLENEAGLES STATION
On 15th May 1964 no. 60004 *William Whitelaw* has an express at Gleneagles station. Photograph by Bill Reed.

*Opposite above* NO. 60004 – STIRLING STATION
No. 60004 *William Whitelaw* is with an express at Stirling station in 1963. Photograph courtesy Colour-Rail.

*Opposite below* NO. 60004 – LEEDS CITY STATION
Aberdeen-based no. 60004 *William Whitelaw* has travelled south to Leeds City station on 19th September 1965 to work the RCTS 'Blyth and Tyne' railtour. Photograph courtesy Colour-Rail.

*Below* NO. 60004 – DARLINGTON SHED
In late June 1965, no. 60004 *William Whitelaw* awaits admittance to Darlington Works for light attention. This would keep the engine in service for another year before withdrawal. Photograph by Bill Reed.

*Opposite above* NO. 60004 – EDINBURGH WAVERLEY STATION

The RCTS and Stephenson Locomotive Society organised a railtour over the weekend of 2nd/3rd June 1962. This was the 'Aberdeen Flyer' which left King's Cross behind no. 60022 *Mallard*. No. 60004 *William Whitelaw* was in charge of the train from Edinburgh Waverley to Aberdeen and a crowd has gathered at the aforementioned station to witness the early afternoon departure. For the return journey, the party used London Midland Region motive power and travelled via the West Coast Main Line. Photograph by Hugh Ballantyne courtesy Rail Photoprints.

*Opposite below* NO. 60004 – GLENEAGLES STATION

Following renaming to *William Whitelaw* in July 1941, no. 60004 (as no. 4462) was transferred from Heaton to Edinburgh Haymarket in an appropriate move given the engine's namesake's Scottish heritage. Born in Dunbartonshire, William Whitelaw was MP for Perth in the early 1890s and was later Chairman of the North British Railway before taking the same position with the LNER. No. 60004 worked from Haymarket until June 1963 when taking a berth at Aberdeen shed and withdrawal occurred in July 1966. The engine would have been no stranger to the Edinburgh-Aberdeen route and is working a southbound express here at Gleneagles station (between Perth and Stirling) on 15th May 1964. Photograph by Bill Reed.

*Below* NO. 60004 – PERTH STATION

No. 60004 *William Whitelaw* has made a stop at Perth station during the mid-1960s. The locomotive has a double chimney, AWS equipment, speed indicator and electricity warning decals. Photograph courtesy Colour-Rail.

**NO. 60005 – EDINBURGH HAYMARKET SHED**
On the turntable at Edinburgh Haymarket during the early 1960s is no. 60005 *Sir Charles Newton*. Photograph by Bill Reed.

*Above* NO. 60005 – PETERBOROUGH STATION

Gateshead's no. 60005 *Sir Charles Newton* approaches Peterborough station with a southbound express on 10th September 1960. Photograph courtesy Colour-Rail.

*Below* NO. 60005 – YORK

No. 60005 *Sir Charles Newton* has the short-lived British Railways blue livery at York during June 1950. The locomotive was in this form from November 1949 to November 1952. Photograph courtesy Colour-Rail.

*Below*

### NO. 60005 – ABERDEEN FERRYHILL SHED

No. 60005 *Sir Charles Newton* presents a sorry sight at Aberdeen Ferryhill shed during mid-1964. The locomotive was withdrawn from the shed in mid-March following just a few months in service there. No. 60005, which has been shorn of much identification (apart from the cabside number), was later sold for scrap to G.H. Campbell at Airdrie. Photograph courtesy Colour-Rail.

*Above* NO. 60005 – DURHAM STATION

No. 60005 *Sir Charles Newton* has a through parcels train at Durham station on 15th July 1961. Whilst several members of the upper hierarchy of the LNER had the honour of their name being carried by an A4, other directors had to settle for a Thompson B1 4-6-0. No. 61237 *Geoffrey H. Kitson* is at the platform as no. 60005 passes by. Photograph by D.J. Dippie.

*Above* NO. 60006 – ABERDEEN FERRYHILL SHED

Aberdeen Ferryhill shed was located just to the south of the city, on the western side of the main line. The turntable was found on the south east boundary between the main building/repair shop and the coal stage. No. 60006 *Sir Ralph Wedgwood* is using the turntable on 8th June 1965 and would have been a regular on the apparatus, being allocated to the depot from May 1964 until condemned in September 1965. The locomotive was later scrapped at Motherwell. Photograph courtesy Colour-Rail.

*Opposite Page* NO. 60006 – ABERDEEN FERRYHILL SHED

No. 60006 *Sir Ralph Wedgwood* is at Aberdeen Ferryhill shed on 17th July 1965 and under preparation for working the 'Grampian' express. This was one of several named trains on the former Caledonian Railway main line between Glasgow and Aberdeen, with the others being the 'Saint Mungo', the 'Bon Accord' and the 'Granite City'. Following the dieselisation of the East Coast Main Line, a number of A4s were unemployed, even though the engines were still highly capable and well-regarded. Several were drafted to Scotland to work between Glasgow and Aberdeen as a result. The fastest scheduled times were set at three hours and were generally well maintained with a 300-ton train over the difficult terrain. The 'Grampian' was the 08.25 departure from Glasgow Buchanan Street station and had stops at Perth and Forfar, before reaching Aberdeen in three hours. The return had an hour extra on the northbound schedule, as several more stops were made, with departure at 13.30. Photograph by Bill Wright.

### *Opposite above* NO. 60006 – MARSHMOOR

A northbound express is at Marshmoor with no. 60006 *Sir Ralph Wedgwood* during August 1955. The locomotive was one of the A4s based in the south to be fitted with the original Automatic Train Control equipment in 1950. The scheme did not progress quickly and was only revived by the tragic Harrow disaster in 1952 when 112 people were killed. Soon after, all A4s in the Eastern Region were equipped and no. 60006 has the new apparatus here.

### *Opposite below* NO. 60006 – PERTH STATION

On a rainy day, 19th August 1964, local enthusiasts have braved the elements to capture the events at Perth station. Two light engines have been found: a Stanier Class 5 4-6-0 and no. 60006 *Sir Ralph Wedgwood*. The latter's streamlined non-corridor tender is shown and this was not original to the locomotive. Tender no. 5670 originally followed no. 60006 – as no. 4466 *Herring Gull* – into traffic and only parted from the engine in late December 1950. For around four year afterwards *Sir Ralph Wedgwood* had a corridor tender (no. 5647) which had been with no. 4492 *Dominion of New Zealand* over the same period. No. 60006's final pairing was with streamlined non-corridor tender no. 5675 that had been built with no. 4900 *Gannet*. Photograph courtesy Colour-Rail.

### *Below* NO. 60006 – KING'S CROSS STATION

Whereas other regions of BR took some time in completing the switchover to diesels, the Eastern Region quickly adopted the Deltic design, amongst others, and had banned steam on much of the southern end of the ECML in mid-1963. Yet, this was still two years away in May 1961 when no. 60006 *Sir Ralph Wedgwood* was captured at King's Cross station ready to take out a northbound express. The shed's staff were also still proud to be turning out the A4s for duties as the engine's condition is immaculate. Photograph courtesy Colour-Rail.

*Above* NO. 60007 – KING'S CROSS STATION

The year 1952 marked the 100th anniversary of the complete opening of the Great Northern Railway line to Doncaster. As part of celebrations to mark this event, a special train was organised to run from King's Cross to York, then returning via the alternative route via Knottingley and Lincoln. No. 60007 *Sir Nigel Gresley* was chosen to work the special and performed well, with nearly 90 mph uphill at Little Bytham with 10 carriages, and reached York just under the 3 hours 15 minute schedule. The locomotive poses here at King's Cross with the Driver and Fireman of no. 60007. Photograph courtesy Colour-Rail.

*Opposite above* NO. 60007 – PERTH STATION

On 15th May 1965, no. 60007 *Sir Nigel Gresley* has made a stop at Perth for water whilst working a southbound express. Following 13 years at King's Cross shed, no. 60007 made a gradual journey northward, with three months at Peterborough from June 1963, then nine months at Edinburgh St Margaret's shed before reaching Aberdeen in July 1964. The locomotive was at work there until February 1966 and was thankfully purchased for preservation. Photograph by Bill Reed.

*Opposite below* NO. 60007 – GLASGOW BUCHANAN STREET STATION

The Caledonian Railway originally ran into Townhead station in Glasgow. Yet this was inadequate and the company extended the line to Buchanan Street station which opened in 1849. Services from London ran into the station but this was too circuitous, being on the north side of the city, and Buchanan Street station subsequently served trains for Aberdeen, Perth etc. Despite being the hub for this traffic, Buchanan Street station was quite small and cramped and, like Queen Street station, was reached via a tunnel, which can be glimpsed here in the distance. The last mentioned station was ultimately deemed more suitable for future requirements and Buchanan Street was closed in 1966. The arrival of the A4s in Scotland added a touch of glamour to the station in these last years and no. 60007 *Sir Nigel Gresley* awaits the departure time of this unidentified express on 21st August 1964. Photograph courtesy Colour-Rail.

*Opposite above* NO. 60007 – PLEAN

Between Stirling and Falkirk at Plean, no. 60007 *Sir Nigel Gresley* works the southbound 'Grampian' express on 7th July 1965. Photograph by Gerald T. Robinson.

*Opposite below* NO. 60007 – STIRLING STATION

The 07.10 departure from Aberdeen to Glasgow was named the 'Bon Accord' and made three stops during the three-hour schedule. The final break in the journey was made at Stirling around 09.29 and no. 60007 *Sir Nigel Gresley* is there with the train on 15th May 1965. Photograph courtesy Colour-Rail.

*Below* NO. 60007

The popularity of the A4s often ensured a class member was used for a special train. Perhaps the most famous instance of this occurred on 23rd May 1959, when no. 60007 *Sir Nigel Gresley* was requested for the Stephenson Locomotive Society's golden jubilee celebrations. The train ran from King's Cross to Doncaster via Lincoln northbound before returning to the capital direct. On this southbound journey, special dispensation was given for the locomotive to take the train, which consisted of eight carriages weighing 295 tons gross, over the 90 mph speed restriction then in force. After passing Grantham, no. 60007 quickly achieved 100 mph and peaked at 112 mph near Essendine. This set the post-war speed record for steam traction. Fireman Hancox and Driver Hoole were at the controls, with the latter particularly famous for his hard-running with A4s during the 1950s. Retiring a short time later in 1959, Driver Hoole poses here with his regular engine no. 60007 (perhaps at King's Cross shed) before working the 'Stephenson Jubilee' special. Photograph courtesy Colour-Rail.

*Above* NO. 60008 – BELLE ISLE

As trains emerged from Gas Works Tunnel there was an open section, which had quite a complicated track layout, owing to the shed, goods station and sidings located on the west side of the main line, before trains disappeared into Copenhagen Tunnel at Belle Isle. This was nearly 600 yards long and was originally just one bore (left as seen here) before the volume of traffic necessitated further lines. The first was built to the west of the original in 1877 and followed by an eastern bore in 1878. These were ultimately arranged, from west to east, to handle goods traffic, northbound trains and services for King's Cross. Film fans will recognise the location from the Ealing comedy *The Ladykillers* (1955) with Alec Guinness. The location for the house the gang meet in was supposedly located at the end of Frederick Street, with the end house visible here, and above Copenhagen Tunnel. Yet, this was just a set, although some exterior scenes did take place above the portals. Interestingly, the view from the front door was not of Frederick Street, but Argyle Street, south of King's Cross and with St Pancras station visible. Here, no. 60008 *Dwight D. Eisenhower* has just emerged from the eastern portal with the 07.18 from Grantham on 1st June 1963. The engine was rapidly approaching the end of a 13-year career working from King's Cross shed. Photograph by Gerald T. Robinson.

*Below* NO. 60008 – GRANTHAM STATION

No. 60008 *Dwight D. Eisenhower* is at the head of an express at Grantham station on 12th July 1962. The locomotive displays King's Cross shed's '34A' shedcode above the middle lamp iron on a plaque. This was introduced by BR in the late 1940s and resulted in the loss of the shed name as part of the livery at the front end, although the class designation remained in various forms. Photograph by Cedric Clayson courtesy John Clayson.

*Above* NO. 60008 – HITCHIN STATION

An uncharacteristically dirty King's Cross A4, no. 60008 *Dwight D. Eisenhower,* approaches Hitchin station with the 07.30 express from Leeds (with a portion from Bradford) to King's Cross on 2nd November 1957. The engine still has a single chimney here but would receive the Kylchap arrangement during a general repair at Doncaster in August 1958. The front end of the locomotive appears to be doing a good job of deflecting the exhaust away from the cab which was a particular consideration during the design of the class. Gresley also had a strong belief that the streamlining would help to achieve reductions in air resistance and promote faster running, specifically uphill, where greater margins of time could be gained over an unstreamlined locomotive. He also thought that streamlining would save power at high speed and calculated nearly 100 horsepower at 80 mph. Photograph by B.W.L. Brooksbank.

*Opposite above* NO. 60008 – DONCASTER WORKS

With the onset of dieselisation in the late 1950s, BR established the Consultative Panel for the Preservation of British Transport Relics to save noteworthy items from stock for the future. These were to be housed in the old LNER Railway Museum at York, or any other establishment that was willing to accept such a gift. The most obvious choice for preservation was no. 60022 *Mallard,* but no. 60008 *Dwight D. Eisenhower* was also selected, although not for Britain. Instead, the locomotive was offered to the American National Railroad Museum in Green Bay, Wisconsin, and accepted. No. 60008 was given just a cosmetic overhaul at Doncaster Works following withdrawal in July 1963 and was transported via the ex-Great Central Railway line to Eastleigh shed, before reaching Southampton on 24th April 1964. Dr Richard Beeching handed the locomotive to the President of the American National Railroad Museum during a ceremony and no. 60008 was then loaded on to the ship *American Planter,* later arriving in Green Bay during late May. No. 60008 *Dwight D. Eisenhower* has been photographed here at Doncaster Works in early 1964 before being dispatched.

*Opposite below* NO. 60008 – KING'S CROSS SHED

An atmospheric view at King's Cross shed on 5th August 1962, with no. 60008 *Dwight D. Eisenhower* in the yard opposite Thompson B1 Class 4-6-0 no. 61318 of Immingham. Photograph courtesy Colour-Rail.

*Above* NO. 60009 – NEWCASTLE STATION

Allocated to Edinburgh Haymarket from new, no. 60009's first transfer occurred in May 1962 when moved to Aberdeen Ferryhill. The latter's '61B' code is on the front of the engine, which is at Newcastle station during 1964 with the 16.30 service to Berwick. No. 60009 is perhaps returning northward following light attention at Darlington during April of that year. Note a crew member is in the tender dousing the coal with water to keep the dust down. Photograph courtesy Colour-Rail.

*Opposite above* NO. 60009 – DUNBLANE

No. 60009 *Union of South Africa* was fitted with several non-standard components during the engine's time in service. The first was the coat of arms of South Africa, which was painted on to a metal plate fixed to the cabside; this resulted in the works plate being moved inside the cab. Secondly, the locomotive received a whistle of the type used by the South African Railways. Finally, a prominent South African businessman presented a plaque depicting a springbok in 1953 and this was fitted, to the right side only, in 1954. The latter is visible here, whereas the whistle was removed during the war and replaced with the Crosby tri-note type used by all A4s. The plate with the coat of arms was left off the engine following the final general repair. No. 60009 *Union of South Africa* is on Dunblane Bank here during May 1964, with the northbound 'St Mungo' express, which was the 17.30 departure from Buchanan Street for Aberdeen and scheduled to pass Dunblane around 18.20 following the stop at Stirling. Dunblane was located on a six-mile long incline with a number of gradients around and below 1 in 100. Photograph by Gerald T. Robinson.

*Opposite below* NO. 60009 – GATESHEAD SHED

Following the takeover of the East Coast Main Line by the Deltics in mid-1963, steam was very rarely allowed south of Peterborough. Dispensation was given for certain organised railtours, such as the 'Jubilee Requiem' organised by the RCTS/SLS on 24th October 1964. This was to be the last steam hauled express to leave King's Cross station, with no. 60009 *Union of South Africa* the engine chosen for this honour. Leaving the capital at 07.55, some five hours was allowed to Newcastle before the ten-coach train returned south at 15.46. On the latter leg, the train had a clear run and was free to attack Stoke Bank, with a high of 95 mph recorded on the falling grade. Here, no. 60009 is at Gateshead shed for servicing between the journeys. Photograph courtesy Colour-Rail.

*Above* NO. 60009 – ABERDEEN STATION

No. 60009 *Union of South Africa* has reached Aberdeen with an express on 4th June 1965. Just less than a year was left in service for the locomotive, as withdrawal occurred in June 1966 when one of the few A4s left in service. In 1967, a farewell was organised for the locomotive with Stanier Class 5 no. 44997 and a heavy train was worked between Perth and Aberdeen, then Perth and Edinburgh Waverley. The locomotive was the subject of a successful private purchase bid by a consortium of investors led by John Cameron. Photograph courtesy Colour-Rail.

*Opposite Page* NO. 60009 – DONCASTER WORKS

Completing a general repair at Doncaster Works in early November 1963, no. 60009 *Union of South Africa* became the final steam locomotive to be overhauled there. As a result, several groups of employees posed with the locomotive to mark the occasion and one is seen here. No. 60009 had been in traffic for 26 years at this point and completed over 1,600,000 miles, many of them at high speed for prolonged periods. The engine had returned to Doncaster for overhaul 19 times and on average went 16 months between major repairs, although eight out of course visits were made to Doncaster along with one to Cowlairs Works, Glasgow. The RCTS *Locomotives of the LNER Part 2A: Tender Engines – Classes A1 to A10* notes that on average A4s were expected to run 80,000 miles or 75,000 for those in Scotland. Yet, *Union of South Africa* exceeded the figure in the early 1950s by completing nearly 127,000 miles and this was the highest recorded by an A4. At the end of steam repairs at Doncaster, an estimated 40,000 had been carried out from the works opening in 1853, whilst some 2,228 steam locomotives had been erected between 1867 and 1957, with no. 60009 works no. 1853.

**NO. 60010 – GRANTHAM STATION**
On 12th July 1962, no. 60010 *Dominion of Canada* is at Grantham station with a northbound freight train. Photograph by Cedric Clayson courtesy John Clayson.

*Above* NO. 60010 – DONCASTER WORKS

No. 60010 *Dominion of Canada* nears the end of the final general repair at Doncaster on 6th June 1963. No. 60007 *Sir Nigel Gresley* was in a similar situation and the top half of the engine's front casing is on the left. Photograph courtesy Colour-Rail.

*Below* NO. 60010 – DONCASTER STATION

For much of the BR period, no. 60010 *Dominion of Canada* carried the bell, yet when the double chimney was fitted there was no space and this feature had to be left off. No. 60010 has stopped at Doncaster station with an express in June 1962. Photograph courtesy Colour-Rail.

*Above* NO. 60010 – DARLINGTON WORKS

Dispatched from Aberdeen to Darlington Works for repair in May 1965, no. 60010 *Dominion of Canada* was condemned instead. The engine was then stored at Darlington shed for over a year (pictured here on 15th November 1965) before shipped to Crewe Works for restoration, as no. 60010 was donated to the Canadian Railroad Historical Association. Photograph by D.J. Dippie.

*Below* NO. 60010 – SUNDERLAND STATION

The 12.03 service from Newcastle to Colchester moves away from Sunderland station behind no. 60010 *Dominion of Canada* on 8th June 1962. Photograph by D.J. Dippie.

*Above* NO. 60010 – DONCASTER WORKS
No. 60010 *Dominion of Canada* is ready to be stripped for repair at Doncaster Works on 26th May 1963. The engine is minus tender no. 5326 which was one of the original corridor tenders and used from new until the end of 1937, only to be reunited with the locomotive in 1960. Photograph courtesy Colour-Rail.

*Below* NO. 60010 – SUNDERLAND STATION
At Sunderland station on 24th April 1960 is no. 60010 *Dominion of Canada*. Photograph by D.J. Dippie.

*Opposite above* NO. 60011 – GRANTSHOUSE

The summer of 1948 was unseasonably wet and when the precipitation intensified on 12th August, the border region was particularly affected. The ECML between Goswick and Scremerston was blocked during the afternoon due to floodwaters, then at night, 11 bridges were swept away between Dunbar and Berwick. Services were seriously disrupted, beginning with the 'Flying Scotsman', which had to detour on to the West Coast Main Line and arrived in Edinburgh some ten hours late. The disruption in the area lasted until November 1948, when all the bridges had been replaced with temporary structures. One of these is visible here in the background, as no. 60011 *Empire of India* approaches with an Edinburgh-bound express on 13th August 1949. The locomotive is decorated in LNER Garter Blue livery with 'British Railways' on the tender, as well as the class designation and shed allocation at the front end.

*Opposite below* NO. 60011 – PERTH STATION

In November 1946 no. 60011 *Empire of India* returned to LNER Garter Blue livery following four years in black. From June 1950 until April 1952, the locomotive had BR blue with dark blue and white lining and had BR green with orange and black lining after the latter date. Initially, no. 60011 had the early BR emblem and during the late 1950s acquired the second version. *Empire of India* is at Perth station on 30th June 1963 taking on water whilst working an express. Photograph courtesy Colour-Rail.

*Below* NO. 60011 – EDINBURGH WAVERLEY STATION

The 10.15 express to King's Cross departs from Edinburgh Waverley station on Saturday, 6th August 1949, behind no. 60011 *Empire of India*. The locomotive has the full-width dust shield across the leading bogie axle and this was a modification carried out in the early 1940s. A by-product of the change required the drain pipes from the middle cylinder to be re-routed alongside those from the outside cylinders. All were supported by the long guard irons, which would later be removed during the early 1950s, causing the pipes to be cut back.

*Above* NO. 60011 – ABERDEEN FERRYHILL SHED

Taking on coal ahead of a Peppercorn Pacific at Aberdeen Ferryhill shed in the summer of 1962 is no. 60011 *Empire of India*. Photograph by Bill Reed.

*Opposite above* NO. 60011 – DONCASTER WORKS

As the A4s accumulated miles during the late 1930s, maintenance was necessary. Certain tasks could be performed at sheds, including changing boiler tubes. Whilst those located lower down were easy to access, tubes higher up were awkward and required the disconnecting of the casing door from the hinge. In doing so, shed staff found that opening the door to the required position made the top lamp bracket foul the whistle. As a result, authority was received for the iron to be lowered by several inches. At the same time, the lower portion of the casing door was disconnected from the mechanism and had to be opened by hand, being supported by chains. No. 60011 *Empire of India* is at Doncaster Works in the early 1950s and had just undergone a general repair. Photograph by Malcolm Crawley.

*Opposite below* NO. 60011 – GLASGOW BUCHANAN STREET STATION

No. 60011 *Empire of India* left Edinburgh Haymarket shed in June 1962 after 24 years there. The engine then spent nearly two years at Aberdeen before withdrawal in May 1964, when dispatched to Darlington for repair. No. 60011 had been kept in traffic up to this point thanks to the efforts of Inverurie Works, north of Aberdeen, following three visits to the shops. *Empire of India* had been there for attention around a month before pictured here, backing on to a northbound train at Glasgow Buchanan Street station, on 7th May 1963. Photograph by Bill Reed.

*Above* NO. 60012 – BLACKFORD HILL (EDINBURGH)

During the early days of the railways, several companies' lines converged at Princes Street, Edinburgh. As traffic on these routes grew rapidly in the second half of the 19th century, a line bypassing this busy bottleneck was deemed necessary. Under the direction of the North British Railway, the Edinburgh Suburban & Southside Junction Railway was established to construct a line from Haymarket to Niddrie. This bypassed the city to the south of Arthur's Seat and opened to traffic, mainly freight, in late 1884. Nearly 80 years later, in June 1964, no. 60012 *Commonwealth of Australia*, has been captured on the line at Blackford Hill (the signal box of the same name is on the right) with a freight train from Millerhill Marshalling Yard, likely to Aberdeen. The engine had been a favourite at Edinburgh Haymarket shed from new until the early 1960s and recorded many notable feats on named passenger services. An example occurred during the flooding crisis of 1948, when no. 60012 worked the 'Flying Scotsman' from King's Cross to Edinburgh non-stop along the revised route, via Carlisle and the Kelso branch, or 408.6 miles. The diversion took the locomotive over severely adverse ground and without facilities to pick up water, making the achievement of a non-stop working particularly noteworthy. Photograph courtesy Colour-Rail.

*Opposite* NO. 60012 – EDINBURGH WAVERLEY STATION

An unusually unkempt Edinburgh Haymarket resident, no. 60012 *Commonwealth of Australia*, is light engine at Waverley station in August 1963. The locomotive had just a few weeks left at the depot, as a transfer to Edinburgh Dalry Road shed was soon to occur. After four months, no. 60012 travelled north to Aberdeen to take a berth there and remained employed until August 1964 when condemned for scrap. Photograph by D.J. Dippie.

*Above* NO. 60012 – EDINBURGH HAYMARKET SHED

No. 60012 *Commonwealth of Australia* is just leaving Haymarket shed for Waverley station on 26th August 1957 to work the 'Elizabethan' express. The engine was in the midst of setting the record for the total number of journeys with the train during a season – 78. Photograph by David Anderson courtesy Rail Photoprints.

*Below* NO. 60012 – PERTH STATION

Passing through Perth station on 10th September 1963 is no. 60012 *Commonwealth of Australia*. Photograph by Bill Reed.

*Above* NO. 60012 – FORFAR STATION

A smoky scene at Forfar station on 10th May 1963, created by no. 60012 *Commonwealth of Australia*. The engine received a double chimney in July 1958 and during 1960 was presented with a whistle of the type used by the Western Australian Government Railways. Photograph by Bill Reed.

*Below* NO. 60012 – NEWCASTLE STATION

Corridor tender no. 5646 is prominent in this view of no. 60012 *Commonwealth of Australia*, taken at Newcastle station on 1st August 1960. Interestingly, the pairing lasted the lifetime of the locomotive. Photograph by D.J. Dippie.

*Above* NO. 60013 – KING'S CROSS SHED
Unsurprisingly, British Railways took some time to decide on the livery of the locomotives. During early 1949, a dark shade of blue was chosen and the first A4 to be transformed from Garter Blue was no. 60013 *Dominion of New Zealand*. The locomotive ran in this livery for nearly three-and-a-half years before receiving BR green with black and orange lining in October 1952, being relatively late in the application of this to the class, as the process began in late summer 1951. No. 60013 *Dominion of New Zealand* is turned at King's Cross shed on 8th January 1961. One of the final batch of Gresley's A3 Class Pacifics, no. 60039 *Sandwich*, is visible on the left. Photograph by Gerald T. Robinson.

*Opposite above* NO. 60013 – DONCASTER STATION
The last carriage of this express is just leaving the main line platform at Doncaster station as no. 60013 *Dominion of New Zealand* gathers speed in August 1956. Gresley D49 4-4-0 no. 62765 *The Goathland* is light engine on the right. Photograph by Geoff Warnes.

*Opposite below* NO. 60013 – FINSBURY PARK
No. 60013 *Dominion of New Zealand* briefly disturbs the work of this track gang at Finsbury Park in June 1954. Photograph courtesy Colour-Rail.

*Above* NO. 60013 – GRANTHAM STATION
No. 60013 *Dominion of New Zealand* makes a stop at Grantham station in September 1957. Photograph by Bill Reed.

*Below* NO. 60013 – EDINBURGH HAYMARKET SHED
When equipped with a double chimney in July 1958, no. 60013 *Dominion of New Zealand* managed to retain the New Zealand Government Railways' whistle. Pictured on 3rd August 1958, the locomotive is leaving Haymarket shed for Waverley station and work on a southbound express. Photograph by David Anderson courtesy Rail Photoprints.

*Above* NO. 60013 – MUSKHAM TROUGHS

Fresh from a general repair and now with a double chimney, no. 60013 *Dominion of New Zealand* is at Muskham water troughs in July 1958. Photograph by Bill Reed.

*Below* NO. 60013 – PETERBOROUGH NEW ENGLAND SHED

One of three A4 withdrawals in April 1963, no. 60013 *Dominion of New Zealand* is at Peterborough New England shed shortly before this event. Photograph courtesy Colour-Rail.

*Above* NO. 60014 – GRANTHAM STATION

Several footplatemen are busy preparing no. 60014 *Silver Link* to work a southbound express from Grantham on 31st August 1961, with a pair of young enthusiasts keeping a keen eye on progress. The locomotive was amongst the class members participating in the early experiments with Automatic Train Control apparatus, receiving the equipment in September 1950. The system, which is visible underneath the drawhook, was effective and tested extensively on the southern half of the ECML during the early 1950s. Yet, the vacuum brake system was found wanting. Gresley had improved the arrangements over the A1/A3 Pacifics by increasing the size of the vacuum cylinders by 3 in. to 21 in. and providing a third, larger cylinder at 24 in. The brake power load was also increased by 30% to 93% of the adhesive weight, though during the ATC tests, A4s travelling at around 90 mph were found to overrun signals by around 600 yards. The bogie stretcher bar required modification due to the fitting of ATC equipment and protection was provided by a square metal plate, avoiding the drawgear swinging down and causing damage. No. 60014 has also lost the long guard irons (removed during July 1953) and this has resulted in the cylinder drain pipes being shortened. The pipes are now supported by a clip attached to the bogie frame behind the leading wheel. Photograph by Cedric Clayson courtesy John Clayson.

*Opposite page* NO. 60014 – GREAT PONTON

Three miles south of Grantham, no. 60014 *Silver Link* has a northbound express at Great Ponton, around 1960. The locomotive was allocated to King's Cross from new until August 1944 and subsequently returned to the capital for good in 1950. No. 60014 had received the BR number in June 1949, at which time BR blue livery was also applied. A change to green was made in January 1952 with the first emblem, yet the second version has since been applied. Photograph by Bill Reed.

*Opposite above* NO. 60014 – RETFORD

View north from the lineside a short distance to the south of Retford station, as no. 60014 *Silver Link* approaches with an express in 1958. Photograph by Bill Reed.

*Opposite below* NO. 60014 – MARYLEBONE STATION

A4s were often favoured for organised excursions during the 1950s and 1960s. No. 60014 *Silver Link* has been selected to work this Ian Allan special on 12th May 1956. The 'Pennine Pullman' train was scheduled to run from Marylebone station and on the ex-Great Central Railway line to Sheffield Victoria, where an electric locomotive was to take over for the crossing of Woodhead. Two Robinson J11 Class 4-4-0s – no. 62662 *Prince of Wales* and no. 62664 *Princess Mary* – were then attached, taking the service via the ex-Lancashire & Yorkshire line (passing Rochdale and Sowerby Bridge) to Barnsley. A rendezvous was made nearby with no. 60014, which conveyed the party back to London on the ECML to King's Cross. Photograph courtesy Colour-Rail.

*Below* NO. 60014 – DONCASTER STATION

No. 60014 *Silver Link* has been sent around the western side of Doncaster station during the early 1960s, as track work is carried out with the help of the shed's breakdown crane. The fireman has taken a fair amount of coal from the tender, which is no. 5590 originally from no. 60015 *Quicksilver*. No. 60014 had undergone several tender changes from the first in January 1936 that saw no. 5589 swapped for no. 5590. In total there were eight changes recorded, with six different tenders, and *Silver Link* used no. 5590 four times. The present pairing lasted from July 1955 until withdrawal in December 1962.

*Opposite above* NO. 60015 – STUKELEY

Travelling through Stukeley, just north of Huntingdon, with an up express on 11th September 1959 is no. 60015 *Quicksilver*. Even with the known benefits of the Kylchap double chimney and blastpipe, the Eastern Region was reluctant to fit the apparatus to engines with a standard chimney. Therefore, experiments were conducted during the early 1950s, using the testing station at Swindon Works, to determine the optimal setting for the A4s' single blastpipe and chimney. No. 60015 was involved and had the blastpipe diameter set at 5⅜ in., with the choke 1 ft 3 in. diameter and the chimney opening 1 ft 4¾ in. In service, this made no appreciable difference and arguments were again made for the Kylchap system; *Quicksilver* received a double chimney in August 1957.

*Opposite below* NO. 60015 – MUSKHAM WATER TROUGHS

No. 60015 *Quicksilver* uses the troughs at Muskham, to the north of Newark, around 1958. The addition of a corridor in the tender was not made at the expense of water capacity, rather that of coal, with 8 tons nominal load compared to 9 tons for the non-corridor tender. Photograph by Bill Reed.

*Below* NO. 60015 – YORK STATION

No. 60015 *Quicksilver* draws a crowd of admirers at York station on 3rd April 1961, as the locomotive makes a stop with a service from Aberdeen to King's Cross. No. 60015 is fitted with King's Cross shed's '34A' shedcode on the smokebox door and the engine's allocation there lasted from September 1951 until withdrawn in April 1963. Photograph courtesy Colour-Rail.

*Above* NO. 60015 – WELWYN

A mid-afternoon express speeds along the ECML near Welwyn on 15th August 1962. The smart engine heading the train is no. 60015 *Quicksilver*. From new the A4s were fitted with French-built Flamen speed recorders, which took a reading from the right-hand rear coupled wheel and relayed the information to an instrument in the cab under the fireman's seat. The speed was also recorded on a sheet of paper contained in a drum roll and this practice lasted until the onset of war, when all were removed. Following the conflict, a small number of engines were refitted with the apparatus, although not until the end of the 1950s, when a driver had misjudged the speed over a restriction, was the decision taken to fit new speed indicators. These were manufactured by Smith-Stone and took the reading from the left-hand rear coupled wheel. No. 60015 was equipped with the type in January 1961 and is visible here. Photograph by D.J. Dippie.

*Below* NO. 60015 – DONCASTER WORKS

This distressing image was captured on 26th May 1963 and shows no. 60015 *Quicksilver* being scrapped at Doncaster Works. The locomotive had been proudly maintained there from new, but became one of fourteen to be cut up by the works (including no. 4469 *Sir Ralph Wedgwood*, which was destroyed in the war) following the displacement of the class by diesel locomotives. No. 60015 was also one of three 'silver' engines disposed of at Doncaster. Photograph courtesy Colour-Rail.

NO. 60016 — GLASGOW ST ROLLOX SHED

One of three A4s caught inside St Rollox shed, Glasgow, on 29th March 1964, no. 60016 *Silver King* awaits attention before returning to service. Photograph by Neville Simms from the Ramwell Collection courtesy Rail Photoprints.

*Above* NO. 60016 – PERTH STATION

The 'West Coast Postal' service from Aberdeen to London has made the scheduled early evening stop at Perth station on 15th May 1964, with no. 60016 *Silver King* at the head of the train. Photograph by Bill Reed.

*Below* NO. 60016 – ABERDEEN FERRYHILL SHED

No. 60016 *Silver King* has been captured near Aberdeen Ferryhill shed on 16th April 1964. Photograph by Bill Reed.

*Opposite above* NO. 60016 – ABERDEEN STATION

Whilst the railways are perhaps thought of as carriers of passengers and freight, the transport of mail was particularly important, if less well-known. On the West Coast Main Line, the premier service was the 'West Coast Postal', which regularly ran in the early evening from London Euston station. The train travelled through the night, collecting and dropping off post from various stations and points lineside, all the way northward to Aberdeen. A reverse service also ran, but left Aberdeen some time earlier at 15.30, with arrival in Glasgow scheduled for 18.25 and a portion from Edinburgh was collected. Carlisle was to be reached by 21.00 and London at 04.00. Various types of motive power were used over the years and the train was latterly entrusted to ex-LNER types, such as the A4s and V2s. No. 60016 *Silver King* is just departing from Aberdeen station here, on 16th April 1964, and would be employed at least until Glasgow, possibly even Carlisle. Photograph by Bill Reed.

*Opposite below* NO. 60016 – PERTH SHED

Nearly two months had elapsed between no. 60016 *Silver King* being withdrawn in late March 1965 and when pictured here at Perth shed. The locomotive had been a long-term resident in the North East from almost new and had spent a number of years subsequently at Gateshead and Heaton sheds. In October 1963, no. 60016 was transferred north to Edinburgh St Margaret's depot, yet was only there a few weeks before travelling further north to Aberdeen. *Silver King* was gainfully employed for another two years and has been transported south for storage at Perth shed, before sold to Motherwell Machinery & Scrap. The nameplate, front numberplate and whistle have all been removed lest they be torn from the carcass by trophy hunters. Photograph by Bill Reed.

*Below* NO. 60016 – NEWCASTLE STATION

Although slightly illegible, someone appears to have written a checklist of inspected components on the left-hand cylinder of no. 60016 *Silver King*. The locomotive, which is at Newcastle station on 24th May 1958, has probably recently undergone a routine examination. This likely found relatively few faults, as no. 60016 remained in traffic until early September before dispatched to Doncaster for a general overhaul. Photograph by D.J. Dippie.

*Above* NO. 60017 – YORK STATION

A southbound express, headed by no. 60017 *Silver Fox,* is at York station on 26th May 1958. Interestingly, the locomotive's nameplate has a red background which was a non-standard appointment, originally only applied to select engines in the late 1930s. This group included the 'silver' engines when they received nameplates, as well as the 'Coronation' five and 'West Riding' pair, with A4s named after distinguished persons also included. This practice was evidently continued for a time under BR, but, as seen with the two images on the left, was discontinued for no. 60017 from at least the early 1960s. Peppercorn A1 Class Pacific no. 60151 *Midlothian* has the standard black nameplate background colour on the right. Photograph courtesy Colour-Rail.

*Opposite above* NO. 60017 – GRANTHAM STATION

A northbound express has stopped at Grantham station c. 1960, with no. 60017 *Silver Fox* leading the train. The engine is perhaps being uncoupled, allowing a gaggle of 'platform enders' to admire *Silver Fox.* Pictured in BR green livery, with second BR emblem, no. 60017 had returned to Garter Blue in September 1947 and was a late recipient of BR blue in September 1950. Just over a year later, the locomotive was wearing BR green. Photograph by Bill Reed.

*Opposite below* NO. 60017 – GRANTHAM STATION

No. 60017 *Silver Fox* slowly moves along the southbound platform at Grantham station on 16th August 1962, as the engine prepares to wait to take over an express to King's Cross. Allocated to the shed there from new until closed in June 1963, no. 60017 subsequently spent just four months at Peterborough New England before sent to Doncaster Works for scrapping. Photograph by Cedric Clayson courtesy John Clayson.

*Opposite above* NO. 60017 – PETERBOROUGH STATION

No. 60017 *Silver Fox* arrives at Peterborough station with a northbound 'Flying Scotsman' service on 18th July 1959. The locomotive was originally provided with corridor tender no. 5592 and this remained coupled through to withdrawal. Only one break occurred in mid-1939 when streamlined non-corridor tender no. 5642 was attached to no. 60017. Photograph courtesy Colour-Rail.

*Opposite below* NO. 60017 – WELWYN NORTH STATION

Before the construction of Welwyn Garden City, the village of Welwyn was provided with a station, around a mile to the east, when the Great Northern Railway opened in 1850. Built with local red bricks, the station was originally known as just Welwyn and was later renamed in 1926 to Welwyn North, following the opening of Welwyn Garden City station. Welwyn North station continues to serve passengers and has been protected with Grade II listed status, being a relatively unmolested example of an original GNR station. No. 60017 *Silver Fox* heads northward through Welwyn with an early evening express on 15th August 1962. Photograph by D.J. Dippie.

*Below* NO. 60017 – GRANTHAM

The turntable at Grantham broke down in the early 1950s and took some time to fix, owing to a failure in the foundations. Yet, further problems in this area saw the apparatus removed altogether and a turning triangle was installed on waste ground immediately west of the shed. No. 60017 *Silver Fox* is on this line on 5th July 1957 with the 'Flying Scotsman' headboard. Photograph by Bill Reed.

**NO. 60018 – GRANTHAM STATION**
Gateshead's no. 60018 *Sparrow Hawk* is at the head of a southbound express in the summer of 1958. Photograph by Bill Reed.

*Above* NO. 60018 – BIGGLESWADE STATION
A northbound express passes through Biggleswade station on 16th April 1961, led by no. 60018 *Sparrow Hawk*. Photograph by B.W.L. Brooksbank.

*Below* NO. 60018 – YORK
In BR blue livery, no. 60018 *Sparrow Hawk* has a southbound 'Flying Scotsman' service at York on 25th April 1950. Photograph by B.W.L. Brooksbank.

*Opposite above* NO. 60018 – NEWCASTLE STATION

No. 60018 *Sparrow Hawk* perhaps offers an example of the other side to the A4 Class. Whereas a number are well-known for their exploits of speed or endurance on named expresses, others went about the day-to-day business of transporting passengers from 'A to B' along the East Coast Main Line without fuss, reliably and punctually. No. 60018 spent 26 years working from the North East, with spells at Gateshead and Heaton over the years, but mainly at the former, and was the first NE Region A4 to be withdrawn in June 1963. The locomotive is with a southbound express and ready to leave Newcastle station on 3rd February 1962. Photograph by D.J. Dippie.

*Opposite below* NO. 60018 – YORK STATION

The driver of no. 60018 *Sparrow Hawk* focuses on the road ahead, as the fireman has a short break in this image captured at York station during 1961. The engine is just passing over the crossing of the ECML and the line from Scarborough at the north end of the station. No. 60018 has taken a fair amount of coal out of the tender (streamlined non-corridor no. 5668, which was always paired with the engine) and likely has been on the train from at least Grantham, with relief perhaps coming at Newcastle, if destined for further north. Photograph courtesy Colour-Rail.

*Below* NO. 60018 – GRANTHAM STATION

No. 60018 *Sparrow Hawk* arrives at Grantham station with an express in the late 1950s. A double chimney is fitted (October 1957), though AWS equipment is not and this task was carried out at Doncaster in November 1958 during an out of course visit to the works. The final addition was a speed indicator which was attached to the engine as part of the final general repair in February 1961. *Sparrow Hawk* had a further two unscheduled visit to works, one to Doncaster in August 1961 and Darlington exactly one year later. Photograph by Bill Reed.

*Above* NO. 60019 – ABERDEEN FERRYHILL SHED
On 2nd June 1966, no. 60019 *Bittern* has been pictured taking coal at Aberdeen Ferryhill shed.  Photograph by Bill Reed.

*Below* NO. 60019 – PERTH STATION
No. 60019 *Bittern* pauses at Perth station during May 1966 with the 17.16 'Granite City' service from Aberdeen to Glasgow. Photograph courtesy Rail Photoprints.

*Above* NO. 60019 – RETFORD
Crossing the River Idle at Retford is no. 60019 *Bittern*, which has a northbound express c. 1960. Photograph by Bill Reed.

*Below* NO. 60019 – GLASGOW BUCHANAN STREET STATION
A train for Aberdeen departs from Glasgow Buchanan Street in May 1966, with no. 60019 *Bittern* making a particularly smoky start. Photograph courtesy Colour-Rail.

*Opposite above* NO. 60019 – SUNDERLAND STATION

No. 60019 *Bittern* moves off from Sunderland station with an express on 26th July 1960. The engine was a long-term resident of the North East before transferred to Edinburgh St Margaret's shed in October 1963. A short time later, no. 60019 moved on to Aberdeen and a further three years were spent in traffic. *Bittern* was one of the final two A4s left in service when withdrawn in September 1966 and was subsequently purchased privately. In recent years, the locomotive has been a regular on the main line working railtours and on preserved routes, though is currently awaiting overhaul. Photograph by D.J. Dippie.

*Opposite below* NO. 60019 – PERTH STATION

Even though a fair amount of water is leaking from the rubber hose connection on the water column, no. 60019 *Bittern* has the tender replenished at Perth station on 7th July 1965. The locomotive carried streamlined non-corridor tender no. 5638 from new through to withdrawal. Photograph courtesy Colour-Rail.

*Below* NO. 60019 – PERTH

Approaching Perth station from the south on 2nd June 1966 is no. 60019 *Bittern*. The locomotive has passed Perth power signal box, which replaced several smaller boxes when opened in 1962, and the old North British Railway engine shed is on the right. This was opened in 1885 and in use until 1950 when closed by BR and turned over to the signals department. Sadly, the building has since been demolished, whilst the signal box remains in use. Photograph by Bill Reed.

*Above* NO. 60020 – EDINBURGH HAYMARKET SHED

With the exception of the fitting of Kylchap double blastpipes and chimneys, the A4 Class received relatively few modifications to the original design over their career. Several minor changes were made at various points to a small number of class members. One concerned the diameter of the middle cylinder which was changed in size from 18½ in. as original to 17 in. Due to the design of Gresley's '2 to 1' lever for operating the middle cylinder, wear could cause unequal work by the three and the reduction in size was an attempt to balance this. Only five engines were modified and the results were inconclusive. No. 60020 *Guillemot* was altered in October 1947 and retained the smaller middle cylinder to withdrawal in March 1964. The engine is outside Edinburgh Haymarket shed around 1960, with classmate no. 60024 *Kingfisher* partially visible on the right. Photograph by Bill Reed.

*Opposite above* NO. 60020 – YORK STATION

Two locomotives prepare to take up their trains at York station on 17th March 1957. No. 60020 *Guillemot* is on the right, whilst Thompson A2/2 Class Pacific no. 60502 *Earl Marischal* is to the left. As no. 4465, *Guillemot* was renumbered 20 as part of the 1946 scheme, taking this in September and also received metal numbers and lettering at the time, along with Garter Blue livery. Two years later, the locomotive took BR number 60020 and from April 1950 wore BR blue until switching to BR green in November 1951. *Guillemot* had been converted to 75% cut-off in mid-1956 and was equipped with a double chimney in late 1957. Photograph courtesy Colour-Rail.

*Opposite below* NO. 60020 – DONCASTER STATION

After the war, there was hope that the LNER's high-speed expresses would be reinstated. This never occurred, but similar services with new names were eventually introduced by the Eastern Region. The 'Tees-Tyne Pullman' replaced the 'Silver Jubilee' in the late 1940s, yet the 'Coronation' did not have a successor until 1957 when the 'Talisman' went into service on the ECML. Departure from both capitals was set at 16.00, with 6 hours 40 minutes allowed for both journeys. The train proved so successful that a morning train was subsequently introduced. No. 60020 *Guillemot* is rushing towards Doncaster station with the northbound 'Talisman' in July 1958. Photograph by Geoff Warnes.

NO. 60020—DREM
East of Edinburgh, on the ECML, loco 60020
*Guillemot* has made a stop at Drem station
during 1955. Photograph courtesy Colour-Rail

*Above* NO. 60020 – YORK SHED
Under the mechanical coaler at York shed in 1964 is no. 60020 *Guillemot*.  Photograph courtesy Colour-Rail.
*Below* NO. 60020
No. 60020 *Guillemot* waits for servicing at an unidentified location, c. 1960.  Photograph courtesy Rail Photoprints.

*Above* NO. 60021 – GRANTHAM STATION

From 1928, the 'Flying Scotsman' ran non-stop between King's Cross and Edinburgh Waverley during the summer months. This feat required a reduced formation, where a larger set was usually required due to the demand of the season. Therefore, a 'relief' train was necessary and followed behind the non-stop, also calling at some stations en route. After Nationalisation, the decision was made to have the 'Flying Scotsman' as a dedicated service all year, whilst the non-stop was to carry on with a different title and new time slot. This was the 'Capitals Limited' which left King's Cross at 09.30 and Edinburgh at 09.45, being timed around 8 hours. In 1953, the year of the accession to the throne of Elizabeth II, the name was changed to the 'Elizabethan' and a gradual increase in the speed of the train was made subsequently. The A4s resumed the high standard of work on the non-stop, which had been interrupted by the war, and no. 60021 *Wild Swan* has the southbound 'Elizabethan' at Grantham station during July 1958. Photograph by Bill Reed.

*Below* NO. 60021 – WELWYN NORTH STATION
No. 60021 *Wild Swan* leads a southbound express through Welwyn North station on 15th August 1962. The locomotive was primarily a King's Cross resident from new, with short spells at Doncaster and Grantham up to mid-1950, until June 1963 when reallocated to Peterborough New England shed. *Wild Swan* was there for only a short time before withdrawn in October and was scrapped at Doncaster. Photograph by D.J. Dippie.

*Opposite above* NO. 60021 – DURHAM STATION

A southbound express passes through Durham station on 16th July 1960, behind no. 60021 *Wild Swan*. Yet to receive a speed indicator (late 1961), the locomotive had the Kylchap double chimney installed in April 1958 and lost the long guard irons in 1953, whilst the first version of the ATC equipment was present from early 1950. Photograph by D.J. Dippie.

*Opposite below* NO. 60021 – PETERBOROUGH STATION

Waiting at the platform at Peterborough station on 22nd May 1957 is no. 60021 *Wild Swan*. The engine used the short-lived 'E' prefix with the 1946 LNER number from February to September 1948. *Wild Swan* was in Garter Blue livery at this time, with metal numbers and letters, following a repaint in April 1947 and had BR blue from March 1950 to August 1951. As mentioned previously, a red background to the nameplate was usually reserved for 'special' locomotives, yet *Wild Swan* has the honour here. No. 60021 also has the works plate, with works no. 1869, in the traditional position on the cabside, which was not the case with all class members as some had the plaque in the cab. Photograph courtesy Colour-Rail.

*Below* NO. 60021 – WELWYN GARDEN CITY

No. 60021 *Wild Swan* is on the fast line at Welwyn Garden City with a King's Cross-bound express during April 1962. The engine was soon to be admitted to Doncaster Works for light attention and a short time later lost corridor tender no. 5651 for no. 5330 of the same type. Even though no. 60021 possessed the vital connection for working the non-stop from 1957, few runs with the train were recorded over the ensuing years and the only spell was in 1958 when 12 journeys were completed. Photograph courtesy Colour-Rail.

### *Above* NO. 60022 – SWINDON SHED

Hampshire Railfans booked no. 60022 *Mallard* for a railtour on 17th March 1963, shortly before the engine's withdrawal in late April. The train ran from Southampton via Salisbury to Swindon, where a tour of the works occurred. No. 60022 is in the shed yard at Swindon in preparation for the return journey. Footplatemen are in the tender busy sorting coal. This was tender no. 5651 which had recently been attached. When no. 60022 was preserved, tender no. 5670 was coupled and later renumbered 5642 in recognition of the one that ran behind the engine during the record-breaking descent of Stoke Bank. Photograph by Hugh Ballantyne courtesy Rail Photoprints.

### *Opposite above* NO. 60022 – STOKE SUMMIT

Over the nearly 30 miles between Peterborough and Grantham, the East Coast Main Line rose to 345 ft above sea level. This was the highest point the route reached south of York and featured several rising gradients travelling towards the last mentioned city, with these being around 1 in 200 and the worst 1 in 178 for around three miles. Whilst northbound trains could find this section difficult, many of the highest recorded speeds from the LNER and BR were achieved travelling southward. No. 60022 *Mallard* has reached Stoke Summit on 19th August 1961 with the 14.25 express from King's Cross to Newcastle. Photograph by Hugh Ballantyne courtesy Rail Photoprints.

### *Opposite below* NO. 60022 – LANGLEY WATER TROUGHS

This dramatic image has been captured at Langley water troughs in June 1962, as no. 60022 *Mallard* raises the water level in the tender. Unless there has been some sort of mechanical failure, or crisis on the footplate, the fireman surely deserves a 'black mark' for not raising the scoop in time and passengers in the leading carriage would surely be complaining if they had the window open. Langley water troughs were the first out of London (27 miles) and 1,780 ft long. Locomotives would slow to around 60 mph to take on water and could collect around 2,000 gallons. The next set were at Werrington (north of Peterborough), some 50 miles away. Photograph courtesy Colour-Rail.

## NO. 60022 – GRANTHAM STATION

No. 60022 *Mallard* is ready to leave Grantham station with a southbound express on 12th July 1962. The engine took on a corridor tender in 1948 and had several up to withdrawal. No. 5651 is present here, although streamlined non-corridor tender no. 5670 would be preserved with the locomotive. Photograph by Cedric Clayson courtesy John Clayson.

## NO. 60022 – DONCASTER STATION

In late October 1952, the first international meeting of the National Model Railroad Association of America was organised by the British Region. The latter had been established in the early 1940s and joined the larger body, with both being dedicated to celebrating modelling of American railroads. York hosted the event and a series of activities were scheduled, including a visit to Doncaster Works. No. 60022 *Mallard* was booked to work the train from York, which was named the '1952 Dream Liner', and the service is pictured here at Doncaster station, as the engine prepares to go to the shed for servicing.

*Below*

## NO. 60022 – KING'S CROSS STATION

As steam drew to a close at the southern end of the ECML, the RCTS and Stephenson Locomotive Society organised a railtour over the weekend of 2nd/3rd June 1962. The 'Aberdeen Flyer' was set to run from King's Cross to Edinburgh with no. 60022 *Mallard* as a non-stop, although a problem with another locomotive on the line scuppered this plan, and from Edinburgh to Aberdeen with no. 60004 *William Whitelaw*. The tour returned via the West Coast Main Line and was hauled by Stanier 'Princess Royal' Pacifics nos 46200 and 46201. Photograph courtesy Rail Photoprints.

*Above* NO. 60023 – DURHAM STATION

A northbound express coupled to no. 60023 *Golden Eagle* comes off the viaduct just to the south of Durham station on 15th July 1961. Photograph by D.J. Dippie.

*Opposite above* NO. 60023 – SUNDERLAND

View northward towards Forfar Street, Monkwearmouth, Sunderland, as no. 60023 *Golden Eagle* passes by with a fish train on 14th October 1960. Photograph by D.J. Dippie.

*Opposite below* NO. 60023 – CADDER YARD

No. 60023 *Golden Eagle* travels past Cadder Yard, north east of Glasgow, with a modest freight train bound for the city on 28th April 1962. Photograph courtesy Rail Photoprints.

*Above* NO. 60023 – COCKBURNSPATH

Just over the border between Scotland and England, and to the south of Dunbar, Cockburnspath bank was a formidable obstacle for trains travelling southward. Over eight miles from Innerwick to Grantshouse, the line rose at a gradient of 1 in 210. Here, in August 1955, no. 60023 *Golden Eagle* drags a train southward. The engine received a double chimney in September 1958 and AWS apparatus was in place from March 1959. The final modification was the addition of a speed indicator in June 1960. No. 60023 would spend time in Scotland before withdrawal, first being allocated to Edinburgh St Margaret's in October 1963, then Aberdeen in May 1964. Photograph courtesy Colour-Rail.

*Opposite page* NO. 60023 – CARLISLE STATION

Two A4s were employed on the Railway Correspondence & Travel Society's 'Three Summit Tour', which took place on 30th June 1963. No. 60023 *Golden Eagle* began the day, taking the 10-coach train out of Leeds City station and northward via the Settle & Carlisle line to the latter place. There, Stanier 'Coronation' Class Pacific no. 46255 *City of Hereford* transported the train further north to Carstairs for a rendezvous with preserved Highland Railway 'Jones Goods' 4-6-0 no. 103 and McIntosh 0-6-0 no. 57581. A short journey was then completed to Auchinleck on the ex-Glasgow & South Western Railway line to Ayr. No. 60004 *William Whitelaw* was waiting there and returned the party to Carlisle. Another change was made for no. 60023 *Golden Eagle* to complete the last section of the tour to Leeds. No. 60023 is waiting to take over at Carlisle here. Photograph courtesy Rail Photoprints.

*Above* NO. 60024 – GLENEAGLES STATION

At Gleneagles station with a southbound express in June 1966 is no. 60024 *Kingfisher*. Photograph by Gerald T. Robinson.

*Below* NO. 60024 – EXMOUTH JUNCTION SHED

No. 60024 *Kingfisher* travelled from Scotland for the Locomotive Club of Great Britain's 'A4 Commemorative Railtour', which occurred on 27th March 1966. The train ran from Waterloo to Exeter St David's station, returning in the late afternoon. No. 60024 is in the yard at Exmouth Junction shed during servicing. Photograph by Gerald T. Robinson.

*Above and Below* NO. 60024 EDINBURGH WAVERLEY STATION

The A4 Preservation Society, later the A4 Locomotive Society Ltd, was formed to purchase an A4 from BR near the end of steam. Several railtours were organised to raise money, which eventually saved no. 60007 *Sir Nigel Gresley*. The 'East Coast Limited' ran from Doncaster to Edinburgh Waverley and back on 21st May 1966, with no. 60024 *Kingfisher* helping the efforts. The locomotive is admired at Waverley following the first leg (above) and backing out for servicing (below). Both photographs by Geoff Warnes.

*Above* NO. 60024 – GLASGOW ST ROLLOX SHED

Until September 1963, no. 60024 *Kingfisher* was only allocated away from Edinburgh Haymarket for seven months and these spells occurred in the late 1930s. The engine was a favourite at the depot and was often specially prepared to work the principal expresses and other important services. No. 60024 moved from Haymarket to Dalry Road initially before reaching St Margaret's at the end of 1963. Employed there for an extended period, *Kingfisher* did not reach Aberdeen Ferryhill until early 1965. The engine has worked a train from there on 22nd August 1965 and travelled to St Rollox shed for servicing. Photograph by Bill Reed.

*Opposite above* NO. 60024 – EDINBURGH WAVERLEY STATION

View from the Mound to the west end of Edinburgh Waverley station on 27th July 1961. No. 60024 *Kingfisher* is emerging from the tunnel driven through the aforementioned earthworks, after preparations for working an express had been completed at Haymarket shed. Poor quality coal appears to have been dumped in the engine's corridor tender, which was 1928-built no. 5329. This had been attached in March 1957 in place of another original example of the type, no. 5331, which was with *Kingfisher* from new in late 1936. Tender no. 5329 was removed in the summer of 1966 and was scrapped with no. 60034 *Lord Faringdon*, whilst the latter's streamlined non-corridor ran with no. 60024 briefly, before the scrapyard claimed the engine as well. Photograph by D.J. Dippie.

*Opposite below* NO. 60024 – FORFAR

A number of A4s carried embellishments and these were fitted at various points in the career of the class. One of the final instances concerned no. 60024 *Kingfisher* in October 1954. At Edinburgh Haymarket shed, the locomotive received two plaques fitted on either side of the boiler depicting a kingfisher. These were presented by Lieutenant A.F. Mortimer on behalf of the crew of HMS Kingfisher, a recently commissioned vessel. The plaques were carried through to withdrawal and one is seen here, as no. 60024 takes on water at Forfar station in July 1965. Photograph courtesy Rail Photoprints.

*Above* NO. 60025 – KING'S CROSS STATION

One hundred years of travel on the Great Northern Railway line was celebrated on 7th August 1950. The first train had run from Maiden Lane temporary station to Peterborough, then via Boston and Lincoln to Doncaster, where a connection was made with the York & North Midland Railway to reach York. No. 60025 *Falcon* departs from King's Cross station with the 'Flying Scotsman' on the anniversary and, thankfully for the passengers, was able to reach York on the direct route subsequently established. A special train – the 'Centenary Express' – was organised to follow the original route, yet this was not hauled by an A4 and, perhaps appropriately, had Thompson A2/1 Class Pacific no. 60113 *Great Northern* as the motive power.

*Opposite above* NO. 60025 – GRANTHAM SHED

A nice splash of colour livens up this otherwise derelict scene at Grantham shed's coal stage on 22nd June 1952. This is provided by no. 60025 *Falcon* which is wearing BR's blue livery. Yet, only six months remained for the scheme, as BR green was applied at the end of the year and *Falcon* was the penultimate A4 with the blue. The engine was second to last in receiving LNER's Garter Blue following the reintroduction after the war, with the visit to the paint shop not occurring until December 1947; no. 60022 *Mallard* was the final A4 in wartime black and not repainted until March 1948. Grantham shed had a mechanical coaler installed in 1938 (out of shot on the left of the locomotive), yet the old stage, which dated from the turn of the century, remained standing and was likely used at busy periods. Photograph courtesy Colour-Rail.

*Opposite below* NO. 60025 – GRANTHAM STATION

No. 60025 *Falcon* has a southbound express at Grantham station around late 1958 to 1959. A double chimney had been fitted to the locomotive in September 1958 and the addition of a speed indicator in June 1960 would be the final modification. No. 60025 has the final version of the AWS equipment, but had been involved in the initial trials and was the first A4 to receive the apparatus in January 1950. At the same time, *Falcon* was modified for 75% cut-off. Photograph by Bill Reed.

*Above* NO. 60025 – BARKSTON STATION

No. 60025 *Falcon* passes the remains of Barkston station with a northbound express during 1960. The station had been opened on 1st July 1867 with the route from Grantham to Lincoln, which left the main line just north of Barkston, after joining the earlier route to Sleaford and Boston. Barkston closed to passengers in February 1955. No. 60025 was mainly a King's Cross engine but had a spell away at Grantham following Nationalisation. At Peterborough New England from mid-June 1963, withdrawal from there occurred in October. Photograph courtesy Colour-Rail.

*Opposite page* NO. 60025 – KING'S CROSS STATION

The adoption of diesel locomotives for express services had been mooted by the LNER in the run up to Nationalisation, yet the state of the system and financial position of the country saw the plans pushed aside. By the mid-1950s, British Railways had been forced to re-evaluate the situation, as increasing losses required drastic action. The British Transport Commission's *Modernisation and Re-Equipment of British Railways*, released in 1955, called for large scale investment in infrastructure to allow greater speeds for improved services. Perhaps the most shocking feature of the proposal was the complete withdrawal of the steam fleet and replacement with diesel locomotives. As the 1950s ended, a number of new classes were being put to work at the southern end of the ECML, including a number of Type 2s for suburban services. One of the engines from this category contrasts with no. 60025 *Falcon* at King's Cross station on 30th July 1961. The year saw the final time A4s would work the 'Elizabethan' before the Deltics took over and in two years' time, steam would have nearly disappeared from this part of the line. Proving a fatal outcome for no. 60025, the locomotive was broken up at Doncaster soon afterwards. Photograph courtesy Colour-Rail.

*Above* NO. 60026 – YORK STATION
BR Standard Class 2-10-0 no. 92168, which has a parcels train, has been held on the through line at York station to allow no. 60026 *Miles Beevor* to get away with the 09.30 Glasgow Queen Street to King's Cross service on 1st June 1963. Photograph by Ian Turnbull courtesy Rail Photoprints.

*Opposite above* NO. 60026 – GLASGOW BUCHANAN STREET STATION
No. 60026 *Miles Beevor* is at Glasgow Buchanan Street station with a northbound express nearly ready to depart on 15th May 1964. The locomotive had arrived in Scotland at St Margaret's shed during October 1963 and moved to Aberdeen in April of the following year. No. 60026 remained employed until December 1965. Photograph by Bill Reed.

*Opposite below* NO. 60026 – MARKHAM MOOR
Around four miles south of Retford, no. 60026 *Miles Beevor* has an express freight train at Markham Moor in October 1959. The locomotive had been the last A4 to receive BR green livery in January 1953 and at the same general repair, the long guard irons were removed. Photograph courtesy Colour-Rail.

*Above* NO. 60026 – CREWE WORKS

Following withdrawal in December 1965, no. 60026 *Miles Beevor* was sold to Motherwell Machinery & Scrap early in 1966. Yet, the A4 Preservation Society was able to arrange for the locomotive to be kept away from the cutter's torch and be transported to Crewe Works. There, no. 60007 *Sir Nigel Gresley* was being restored and in need of spare parts, which were taken from no. 60026. The remains of the latter were then discarded and sold again to a scrapyard. Behind *Miles Beevor* is BR Standard Class 8 Pacific no. 71000 *Duke of Gloucester*, which was later saved from Barry scrapyard and returned to steam. Here, the engine has the cylinders and rotary cam valve gear removed, as the components were put on display in a museum. Photograph courtesy Colour-Rail.

*Opposite above* NO. 60026 – GREAT PONTON

In May 1960, no. 60026 *Miles Beevor* has an express at Great Ponton near Grantham. Photograph by Bill Reed.

*Opposite below* NO. 60026 – GRANTHAM SHED

Several spells at King's Cross were counted amongst no. 60026 *Miles Beevor*'s allocation history, in addition to periods at Haymarket, Gateshead, Doncaster and Grantham from new until the mid-1960s transfer to Scotland. The final allocation to King's Cross lasted from September 1951 until June 1963 when the depot closed. No. 60026 is at Grantham shed for servicing in May 1960. Photograph by Bill Reed.

*Opposite above*
## NO. 60027 – MARSHALL MEADOWS

In taking over from the non-stop 'Flying Scotsman' in 1949, the 'Capitals Limited' was given the relatively new set of carriages from that train. The 'Flying Scotsman' then had to 'make do' with a new, but slightly austere, formation. The arrangement of the 'Capitals Limited' had two carriages leading for Aberdeen – a third brake and a composite – followed by the remainder for Edinburgh – five third class, including one with a Ladies' retiring room, a buffet, an open third, kitchen, open first, a first class and a bogie van. For the 1952 season, there were slight changes and the formation lost a third, open first and kitchen car in the Edinburgh portion, with the latter two replaced by a single restaurant first carriage, and the Aberdeen section was changed to a composite brake and a third class vehicle. No. 60027 *Merlin* has the southbound 'Capitals Limited' at Marshall Meadows, near the border of England and Scotland, on 25th July 1952.

*Opposite below*
## NO. 60027 – NEWCASTLE STATION

No. 60027 *Merlin* is coming off/going on a train at Newcastle station on 10th February 1962. Recently returned to service following the final general repair, a speed indicator and AWS equipment had been fitted to the locomotive in mid-1960 during the previous visit to Doncaster Works. Photograph by D.J. Dippie.

*Below* NO. 60027 – PERTH

The driver has a good look to the rear as no. 60027 *Merlin* reverses at Perth, perhaps to the shed, during the mid-1960s. Photograph by Bill Reed.

NO. 60027 – PERTH
An express is at Perth with no. 60027 *Merlin* on 15th
May 1964.  Photograph by Bill Reed.

*Above* NO. 60027 – CARLISLE STATION

Gresley A3 Pacific no. 60052 *Prince Palatine*, which was one of the last class members left in service, unfortunately developed a hot axlebox whilst working this special touring the Border region on 5th June 1965. Thankfully, no. 60027 *Merlin* was on hand to take the train back to Edinburgh, via the Waverley route. Photograph courtesy Rail Photoprints.

*Below* NO. 60027 – PERTH STATION

A northbound express has paused with no. 60027 *Merlin* at Perth station on 16th May 1964. Photograph by Bill Reed.

*Above* NO. 60028 – HADLEY WOOD
An express freight is northbound at Hadley Wood around 1960, with no. 60028 *Walter K. Whigham* leading the way. Photograph courtesy Rail Photoprints.

*Below* NO. 60028 – NEWCASTLE STATION
The 'Tees-Tyne Pullman' is ready to leave Newcastle for King's Cross behind no. 60028 *Walter K. Whigham* on 24th May 1961. Photograph by D.J. Dippie.

*Above* NO. 60028 – HARMER GREEN

No. 60028 *Walter K. Whigham* emerges from Welwyn North tunnel at Harmer Green with a down express freight on 31st May 1958. The engine had possessed a double chimney for over six months.

*Below* NO. 60028 – LITTLE PONTON

Climbing to Stoke tunnel, no. 60028 *Walter K. Whigham* will soon be free to run easily down to Peterborough station with the 'Tees-Tyne Pullman', likely during mid-1949. Peppercorn A1 no. 60139 is northbound at Little Ponton and yet to be named. Interestingly, the latter would take no. 60028's old name *Sea Eagle* in May 1950. Photograph courtesy Rail Photoprints.

*Above* NO. 60028 – STOKE SUMMIT

The 'Northumbrian' was another new train introduced by BR in 1949, though both the northbound and southbound services had their origins earlier. Running between King's Cross and Newcastle, the down train was started as a relief to the 13.00, which had grown substantially after the outbreak of war. The up service dated from North Eastern Railway-days and left the north at 10.30. From 1949, the King's Cross departure was made earlier at 12.20 and was allowed just under six hours to reach Newcastle. The 'Northumbrian' left the latter city at 10.40 and had a similar schedule. Both trains stopped at several stations along the line and the load was normally 13 coaches. No. 60028 *Walter K. Whigham* has just reached Stoke Summit with the northbound service on 30th July 1951.

*Opposite above* NO. 60028 – NEWCASTLE STATION

Whilst the 'Elizabethan' ran non-stop during the week, on Saturday the coaches made a stop at Newcastle, although the headboard should have been removed or turned backwards. The set was not used on Sundays, yet the locomotives rostered to work in the week still made the journey with a different formation of carriages. No. 60028 *Walter K. Whigham* has made the Newcastle stop with a Saturday train on 5th September 1961 and the crew are in the tender re-arranging the coal. During the year, the locomotive was a favourite of King's Cross and made as many as 34 journeys with the 'Elizabethan', coming second to no. 60014 *Silver Link*'s total of 41. No. 60028 had been used during three other seasons – 1953, 1956 and 1959 – and had a respectable total of at least 118 journeys with the train. Photograph by D.J. Dippie.

*Opposite below* NO. 60028 – SELBY STATION

No. 60028's prowess with the 'Elizabethan' was only possible due to the engine's corridor tender. One of the original types (no. 5330) had been paired with the locomotive when new until 1945, at which time another from that group (no. 5327) was substituted. For a year beginning June 1951, *Walter K. Whigham* had streamlined non-corridor tender no. 5642 before changing to corridor no. 5649 which was coupled until December 1962, when amongst the first A4 withdrawals. No. 60028 is passing through Selby station with a nameless express in September 1962. Photograph by R.A. Whitfield courtesy Rail Photoprints.

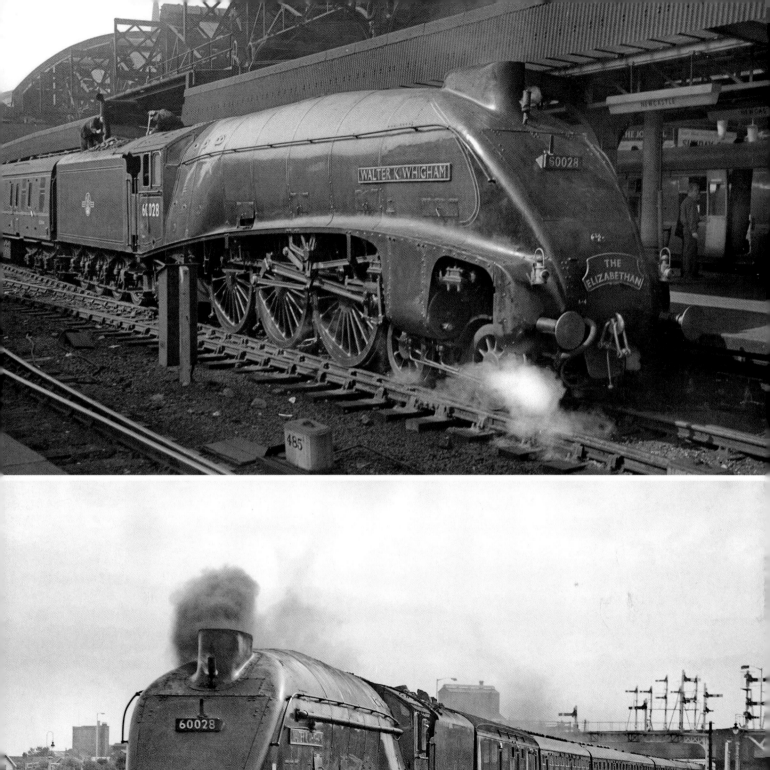

NO. 60029 – DONCASTER SHED

In October 1958, no. 60029 *Woodcock* has just emerged from Doncaster Works following a general overhaul, during which a double chimney was fitted. Ivatt J6 Class 0-6-0 no. 64271 is on the left and has arrived for scrapping. Photograph by Bill Reed.

*Above* NO. 60029 – DONCASTER WORKS

No. 60029 *Woodcock* is at Doncaster Works during 1963. The engine arrived for attention in mid-summer, yet withdrawal occurred in October and no. 60029 was scrapped there soon after. Photograph courtesy Colour-Rail.

*Below* NO. 60029 – BAWTRY

A northbound express is at Bawtry, just south of Doncaster, around 1960, with no. 60029 *Woodcock* leading. For 20 years from 1943, the engine worked from King's Cross shed. Photograph by Bill Reed.

*Above* NO. 60029 – MARSHMOOR

Following Nationalisation, BR experimented with potential new liveries for express passenger locomotives. Classes from across the regions received these schemes, with four members of the A4 class given purple with red cream and grey lining. No. 60029 *Woodcock* was one, along with no. 60024 *Kingfisher*, no. 60027 *Merlin* and no. 60028 *Walter K. Whigham*. The first mentioned was the final A4 in the livery, being repainted from Garter Blue in July 1948. Other schemes considered included a light green, a dark green (similar to the Great Western Railway green and that later adopted by BR) and dark blue. The latter was ultimately selected and no. 60029 was the first of the quartet repainted in January 1950. *Woodcock* has been caught in the purple livery, which had the lining following the running plate, whilst at the head of the northbound 'Yorkshire Pullman' at Marshmoor on 25th August 1949.

*Below* NO. 60029 – YORK STATION

An express has made a stop at York station on 9th June 1957. No. 60029 *Woodcock* is the motive power and stands resplendent at the head of the train. King's Cross shed had a reputation for cleanliness of the locomotives allocated there and was even known to quickly clean locomotives substituted at short notice on expresses. No. 60029 has the non-standard red background to the nameplate. Photograph courtesy Colour-Rail.

*Above* NO. 60030 – SUNDERLAND

View north west from Burdon Road, Sunderland, as no. 60030 *Golden Fleece* departs from the station with the 12.06 Newcastle to Colchester service on 7th June 1962. Two routes connected at the south end of Sunderland station. The route on the left, which has Gresley V3 Class 2-6-2T no. 67688 and a DMU, curved westward to join the 'old main line' between Darlington and Gateshead, with connections to Washington and Durham. No. 60030 is taking the eastbound line that forked Ryhope into the Durham Coast line – running via Hartlepool and Stockton-on-Tees – and the ex-Durham & Sunderland Railway. Since this image was taken, the view to Sunderland station has been blocked by the erection of a modern building housing shops. Photograph by D.J. Dippie.

*Opposite above* NO. 60030 – ARLESEY AND HENLOW STATION

No. 60030 *Golden Fleece* races through Arlesey and Henlow station with the down 'Northumbrian' on 24th June 1954. Photograph by Alan Barkus courtesy Rail Photoprints.

*Opposite below* NO. 60030 – NEWCASTLE STATION

Quite late in the 1961 season of the 'Elizabethan', no. 60030 *Golden Fleece* made a first appearance on the train for the year. This occurred on 11th August as the locomotive took over from no. 60014 *Silver Link* for several days. For the week beginning 21st August, the latter was on the 'Elizabethan', working with no. 60009 *Union of South Africa*. No. 60030 was then back on the roster for the Sunday service before taking out the first southbound train of the new week, which was to end badly for *Golden Fleece*. A mechanical issue forced the engine off the train at Newcastle on Thursday and an A3 took the 'Elizabethan' forward. No. 60030 *Golden Fleece* stands at the head of the 17.00 train from Newcastle to King's Cross on 31st August 1961 following the failure on the northbound 'Elizabethan' earlier in the day. Evidently, the issue was not serious enough for the engine to be held at Gateshead for attention, or to subsequently enter Doncaster Works. *Golden Fleece* had been in the latter recently for a general repair, which was completed at the end of July, and during this, a speed indicator had been fitted. The locomotive would return to Doncaster briefly at the end of 1961 and visit twice during 1962, before withdrawal late in the year. Photograph courtesy Colour-Rail.

*Opposite* NO. 60030 – GRANTHAM STATION

A smart set of coaches with carmine and cream livery stand behind no. 60030 *Golden Fleece* at Grantham during June 1958. The locomotive started the summer season of the 'Elizabethan' on 9th June by taking the down train out of King's Cross, with no. 60031 *Golden Plover* on the up service. No. 60030 worked the 'Elizabethan' for three weeks subsequently before relieved. Several attempts were made to re-establish *Golden Fleece* on the train, yet mechanical problems stopped this from happening. Nevertheless, the locomotive completed a creditable 30 journeys with the 'Elizabethan'. Photograph by Bill Reed.

*Below* NO. 60030 – DONCASTER WORKS

No. 60030 *Golden Fleece* is coming to the end of a month under the care of Doncaster Works and is standing adjacent to the Crimpsall Repair Shop on 25th August 1962. Attention appears to be focussed on the piston valves on both sides and the engine could be at Doncaster for the no. 6 (36,000) mileage examination. P. N. Townend, in his excellent book *Top Shed*, relates that from 1957, all of the Pacifics at King's Cross shed were sent to the shops for this to be carried out. The reasoning was several parts often had to be renewed at this point and there would be a delay waiting for them to be sent south from the works, so for the ease of all concerned, the locomotive was dispatched. Photograph courtesy Colour-Rail.

*Above* NO. 60031 – EDINBURGH WAVERLEY STATION

The 'Capitals Limited' departs from Edinburgh Waverley station behind no. 60031 *Golden Plover* on 6th August 1949. A high standard of reliability had been established by the locomotive on the 'Coronation' before the war and continued with the 'Capitals Limited' and 'Elizabethan' during the 1950s. With the latter train, no. 60031 only missed appearing in three seasons – 1956, 1957 and 1960 – and made sizeable contributions to most years, with 1961 being the highest at over 30.

*Opposite above* NO. 60031 – GLASGOW ST ROLLOX SHED

Whilst several A4s were allocated to Aberdeen, a very small number – two – worked from the Glasgow end of the line. One of these was no. 60031 *Golden Plover*, which stands inside the depot on 29th March 1964; the other was no. 60027 *Merlin*. The aforementioned arrived at St Rollox shed in February 1962 and had three-and-a-half years there, whilst the latter survived for just over two years. The ex-London Midland & Scottish Railway drivers were initially suspicious and derogatory to the rival locomotives, though the A4s soon demonstrated the class had more than enough to match any LMSR designs. Other ex-LNER engines allocated to St Rollox included Gresley A3 and V2s for various periods. No. 60031 is in the company of no. 60016 *Silver King* and an unidentified Peppercorn Pacific. Photograph by Neville Simms from the Ranwell Collection courtesy Rail Photoprints.

*Opposite below* NO. 60031 – PERTH STATION

A small conference of footplatemen appears to be taking place at Perth station on 26th August 1965, while no. 60031 *Golden Plover* takes on water before continuing towards Aberdeen. The locomotive was just one of two A4s that had the diagonal yellow stripe painted on the cab side to denote the engine was barred from working under the electrified lines south of Crewe. The other was no. 60027 *Merlin* and the fact both were St Rollox-allocated perhaps explains why they were so treated, although the likelihood of a journey that far south would surely have been extremely remote. Photograph by Geoff Warnes.

*Opposite above* NO. 60031 – PERTH STATION

Just two months remained in traffic for no. 60031 *Golden Plover* when pictured at Perth station about to take on water in mid-August 1965. One of a small number to visit Cowlairs Works, Glasgow, for attention, no. 60031 had been in the shops just two weeks earlier. The engine had also visited the works a year before over a two-day period, whilst the last general repair had been completed at Doncaster in July 1963. Photograph by Bill Reed.

*Opposite below* NO. 60031 – GALASHIELS STATION

The Stephenson Locomotive Society and the Branch Line Society organised a series of railtours over four days from 16-19th April 1965 that took in a number of places of interest across Scotland. Several locomotives were involved including: Hughes 'Crab' Class 2-6-0 no. 42739; preserved Highland Railway Jones Class 4-6-0 no. 103; preserved Caledonian Railway 'Single' no. 123; preserved Great North of Scotland Railway F Class 4-4-0 no. 49 *Gordon Highlander*; two BR Standard Class 2 2-6-0s, nos 78046 and 78054. On the third day, 18th April 1965, no. 60031 *Golden Plover* was the motive power for a journey from Glasgow Queen Street station to Edinburgh, then Carlisle via the Waverley Route, returning on the West Coast Main Line. Here, no. 60031 is with the train at Galashiels station. Photograph courtesy Colour-Rail.

*Below* NO. 60031 – PERTH STATION

Whilst pictured with a southbound train from Aberdeen (via Dundee) in the image at the top of page 226, no. 60031 *Golden Plover* has been caught again on 20th August 1965, this time travelling northward. Photograph by Bill Reed.

*Above* NO. 60032 – KING'S CROSS SHED

No. 60032 *Gannet* is under the coaler at King's Cross shed on 2nd June 1962; a Peppercorn Pacific is on the adjacent road. Photograph by Gerald T. Robinson.

*Below* NO. 60032 – HOLLOWAY

A northbound express passes under the Caledonian Road bridge at Holloway on 18th August 1962, with no. 60032 *Gannet* leading the way. Photograph by Gerald T. Robinson.

*Above* NO. 60032 – HOLME

On 14th April 1957 no. 60032 *Gannet* conveyed the 'Charnwood Forester' Railtour from King's Cross to Holme station, south of Peterborough. From there, the party toured several local lines before returning to London from Hitchin by no. 60032. Photograph courtesy Colour-Rail.

*Below* NO. 60032 – LEEDS

No. 60032 *Gannet* proceeds with extreme caution at an unspecified location in the Leeds area on 1st June 1963. Photograph courtesy Colour-Rail.

*Opposite above* NO. 60032 – WELWYN GARDEN CITY

The southbound 'Elizabethan' has just passed through Welwyn Garden City station on 17th August 1960. No. 60032 *Gannet* is set to complete another journey between the capitals and would amass 68 during the season. Photograph by D.J. Dippie.

*Opposite below* NO. 60032 - STUKELEY

King's Cross-allocated no. 60032 *Gannet* speeds northward with an express on 11th September 1959. The engine had been fitted with a double chimney for almost a year and in 1960 would receive a speed indicator.

*Below* NO. 60032 – SELBY

By the 1880s, the Hull & Selby Railway's bridge over the River Ouse at Selby had become inadequate for the increased train loads prevailing. A new bridge was commissioned by the successor North Eastern Railway and in use by 1891. This was of the 'swing' type and rotated out of the way of passing river traffic, whilst the original was a 'bascule' bridge, where the sections lifted vertically. The bridge proved somewhat of a bottleneck for ECML traffic and, as well as problems created by the exploitation of the Selby coalfield, resulted in the Selby diversion, opened in 1983. Here, no. 60032 *Gannet* slowly passes over the bridge with a northbound express during 1957. Photograph courtesy Rail Photoprints.

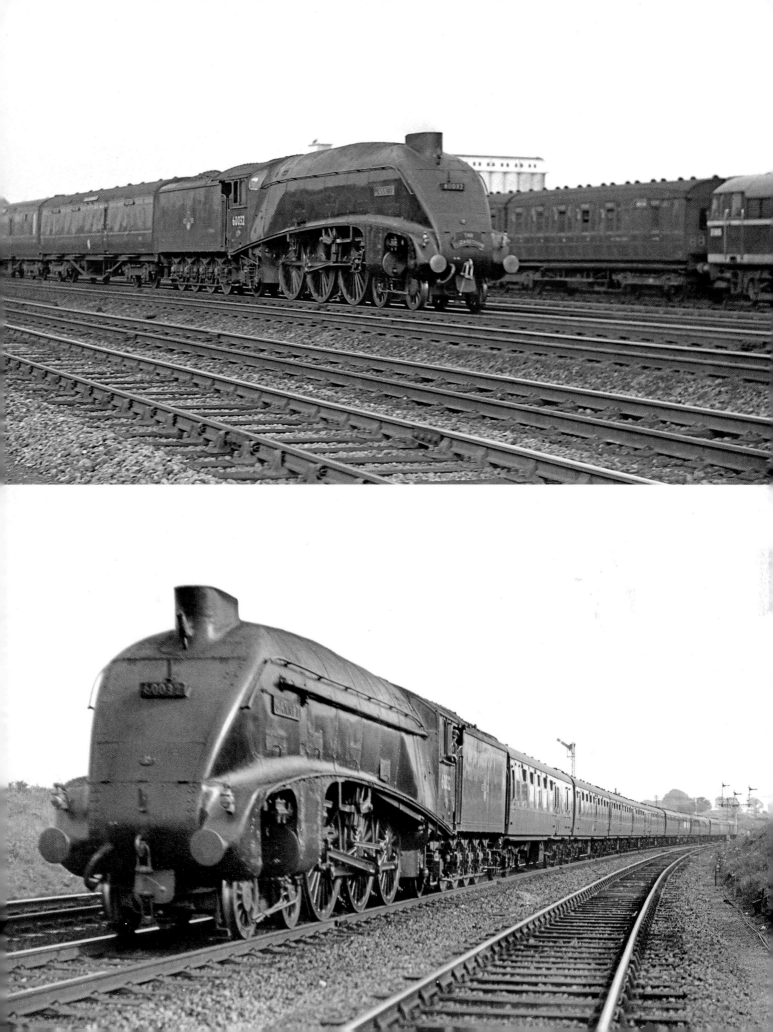

*Above* NO. 60033 – GRANTHAM STATION

As a group of railwaymen take a break for a cigarette, no. 60033 *Seagull* is ready to proceed with the 'Northumbrian' to the next stop at York in July 1956. Photograph by Bill Reed.

*Opposite* NO. 60033 – DONCASTER WORKS

The A4s were well-maintained in the pre-war years and class members were expected to reach 75,000-80,000 miles before a general repair could be undertaken. Yet, the war years and the immediate aftermath seriously undermined this figure and by the early 1950s the average annual mileage of the class was between 52,000-56,000 miles. This figure improved as the decade progressed, as materials became more plentiful and both workshop and shed practices returned to the pre-war level. At Doncaster, the arrival of K.J. Cook, as Mechanical & Electrical Engineer of the North Eastern and Eastern Regions, saw the introduction of optical alignment methods. This helped to reduce stresses caused by high tolerances in the positioning of cylinders, frames, axleboxes, etc. Furthermore, the design of the 'big end' bearing was improved successfully, in partnership with vigilant inspection and maintenance, reducing instances of the bearing running 'hot'. As mentioned previously, sending the A4s at King's Cross back to Doncaster for the 36,000 miles examination also helped and by the late 1950s, several A4s were able to run 100,000 miles between general repairs and even more in some instances. No. 60033 *Seagull* is coming to the end of a three-week visit to Doncaster for light attention on 8th October 1961. The engine appears to have undergone some work, at least to the left-hand cylinder, whilst the connecting wire for the AWS equipment is loose and held to the locomotive by a piece of string. Photograph courtesy Colour-Rail.

*Above* NO. 60033 – KING'S CROSS STATION

No. 60033 *Seagull* is prepared to take a northbound express away from King's Cross station on 20th November 1961. A month had elapsed from the engine's return to traffic following a spell at Doncaster (see p. 232) and King's Cross depot's cleaners no doubt had a hand in restoring the paintwork to an acceptable standard. BR green replaced blue from June 1952 and the latter was used from November 1950. Photograph courtesy Colour-Rail.

*Opposite above* NO. 60033 – ST NEOTS

Following a busy summer in 1956 working the 'Elizabethan', no. 60033 had a quieter year in 1957 and was not used on the non-stop. Gainful employment was found for the locomotive elsewhere and *Seagull* has the southbound 'Northumbrian' at St Neots on 9th September. No. 60033 had been fresh from Doncaster for the exploits in 1956 and would not return to works again until January 1958.

*Opposite below* NO. 60033 – PADDINGTON STATION

Ultimately, the 1948 Exchange Trials were of little practical value for BR's development of the Standard Classes, but they provided data on the classes that took part and might have been otherwise unavailable. The tests also provided good publicity and a talking point for enthusiasts across the country. In the express passenger class category for the trials, the A4s competed against two other Pacific classes – LMSR 'Coronation' and Southern Railway 'Merchant Navy' – as well as a pair of 4-6-0 classes – LMSR 'Royal Scot' and Great Western Railway 'King'. Three A4s were initially selected, no. E21 *Wild Swan*, no. 25 *Falcon* and no. 26 *Miles Beevor*, yet the selection was soon overruled and three Kylchap-fitted locomotives substituted. No. E22 *Mallard*, no. 60033 *Seagull* and no. 60034 *Lord Faringdon* were prepared for the trials, which were carried out between mid-April and late May. No. E22 *Mallard* was ready to take the tests on the Western Region but 'ran hot' on a preliminary run and was substituted by no. 60033 *Seagull*. The trial was conducted on the 13.30 from Paddington to Plymouth, with a train weighing over 480 tons, and the return the next day. Over the week, the locomotive performed well on the difficult route and recorded favourable coal figures against the other locomotives. The A4s were particularly efficient in terms of coal used for the work performed and noted as very free steamers, with little loss of pressure between the boiler and cylinders. No doubt this was attributable to the Kylchap exhaust system and the streamlined steam passages. No. 60033 *Seagull* arrives at Paddington station on 7th May 1948.

## NO. 60034 – PERTH STATION

Tender no. 5640 has the water level topped up during the stop at Perth, whilst no. 60034 *Lord Faringdon* rests with the 08.25 Glasgow to Aberdeen service on 19th July 1966. The tender had been with the engine for just a short period, being first attached in January 1963, replacing corridor tender no. 5325. Photograph by Bill Wright.

*Above* NO. 60034 – KING'S CROSS SHED
No. 60034 *Lord Faringdon* prepares to move off King's Cross shed on 8th January 1961. Photograph by Gerald T. Robinson.
*Below* NO. 60034 – PERTH STATION
The southbound 'Grampian' has made the Perth stop in July 1966, with no. 60034 *Lord Faringdon*. The engine has maintained a presentable appearance, although the wash-out plug covers have been lost. Photograph courtesy Rail Photoprints.

*Opposite above* NO. 60034 – WOOLMER GREEN

A month following a general repair, no. 60034 *Lord Faringdon* has a train bound for Cambridge at Woolmer Green on 13th June 1959. Doncaster works fitted a new boiler to the locomotive and this was one of twenty-five new diagram 107 types built between 1959 and 1961. Interestingly, as no new boilers were authorised to be built for the A3 Class, several A4 boilers, both new and old, were used with the older Gresley Pacifics.

*Opposite below*
NO. 60034 – GLASGOW ST ROLLOX SHED

Looming imposingly over St Rollox shed, Glasgow, is the Red Road housing development, which began construction in 1964 and was completed in 1971. On 22nd August 1965, no. 60034 *Lord Faringdon* is serviced before returning northward with an express for Aberdeen. Also in the yard is Stanier Class 5 no. 44718. Photograph by Bill Reed.

*Below* NO. 60034 – ABERDEEN FERRYHILL SHED

The vacuum pipe from no. 60034 *Lord Faringdon* is connected to the motor for the turntable at Aberdeen Ferryhill shed during 1965. The engine had been a long-term resident of King's Cross depot from 1948 until June 1963 and moved briefly to Peterborough New England before reaching Edinburgh St Margaret's. Seven months later, *Lord Faringdon* arrived at Aberdeen and worked from there until withdrawn in August 1966. Photograph courtesy Colour-Rail.

# BIBLIOGRAPHY

Allen, C.J. *British Pacific Locomotives*. 1975.
Allen, C.J. *The Gresley Pacifics of the LNER*. 1950.
Allen, C.J. *The Locomotive Exchanges*. 1950.
Allen, C.J. *Titled Trains of Great Britain*. 1983.
Aylard, John, Tommy Knox and David Percival. *What's on the 'Lizzie'?* 2010.
Banks, Steve and Clive Carter. *LNER Passenger Trains and Formations 1923-67 – The Principal Services*. 2013.
Bonavia, Michael R. *A History of the LNER: 2 The Age of the Streamliners, 1934-39*. 1985.
Bonavia, Michael R. *A History of the LNER: 3 The Last Years, 1939-48*. 1984.
*British Railways Magazine: Eastern Region* - Various Issues.
Brooksbank, B.W.L. *Triumph and Beyond: The ECML 1939-1959*. 1997.
Brown, F.A.S. *Nigel Gresley: Locomotive Engineer*. 1975.
Griffiths, Roger and John Hooper. *Great Northern Railway Engine Sheds Volume One: Southern Area*. 2001.
Griffiths, Roger and John Hooper. *Great Northern Railway Engine Sheds Volume Three: Lancashire and Yorkshire*. 2000.
Griffiths, Roger and Paul Smith. *The Directory of British Engine Sheds and Principal Locomotive Servicing Points: 2 North Midlands, Northern England and Scotland*. 2000.
Hale, Don. *Mallard: How the 'Blue Streak' Broke the World Speed Record*. 2005.
Harris, Michael. *Gresley's Coaches*. 1973.
Hughes, Geoffrey. *A Gresley Anthology*. 1994.
Knox, Harry. *Haymarket Motive Power Depot, Edinburgh*. 2011.
*LNER Magazine* - Various Issues.
McIntosh, David. *Mallard and the A4 Class*. 2008.
Mullay, A.J. *Non-Stop! London to Scotland Steam*. 1989.
Mullay, A.J. *Streamlined Steam*. 1994.
Nock, O.S. *The Gresley Pacifics Part 1: 1922-1935*. 1973.
Nock, O.S. *The Gresley Pacifics Part 2: 1935-1974*. 1974.
Pike, S.N. *Mile by Mile on the LNER*. 1951.
Quick, Michael. *Railway Passenger Stations in Great Britain: A Chronology*. 2009.
RCTS. *Locomotives of the LNER Part 2A: Tender Engines - Classes A1 to A10*. 1978.
Rutherford, Michael. *Mallard: The Record Breaker*. 1988.
Semmens, P.W.B. *Bill Hoole: Engineman Extraordinary*. 1974.
*The Gresley Observer. 'The Silver Jubilee Commemorative Issue'*. Autumn 1975.
Townend, P.N. *Top Shed*. 1989.
Townend, P.N. *LNER Pacifics Remembered*. 2014.
Tuffrey, Peter. *A4 Pacific Locomotives*. 2016.
Welch, Michael S. *Memories of Steam from Glasgow to Aberdeen*. 2012.
Yeadon, W.B. *Register of LNER Locomotives: Gresley A4 and W1 Classes*. 2001.
Yeadon, W.B. *Register of LNER Locomotives: Appendix Two – Locomotive Tender Numbering*. 2005.

---

Also available from Great Northern

The Last Years of Yorkshire Steam

The Golden Age of Yorkshire Railways

Gresley's A3s

Peppercorn's Pacifics

London Midland Steam 1948-1966

The Last Years of North East Steam

British Railways Standard Pacifics

Western Steam 1948-1966

The Last Years of North West Steam

Gresley's V2s

Southern Steam 1948-1967

Yorkshire Steam 1948-1967

Gresley's B17s

John Ryan's Express

visit www.*greatnorthernbooks.co.uk* for details.